ONE SOLDIER'S WAR

IN HIS OWN WORDS

PFC ALTON S. HAIGHT

Three years in the life of a soldier

NORTH AFRICA AND EUROPE 1942–1945

Other books by Rita M. Boehm

Missing on Maple Street

The Second Chances Trilogy:

- *Second Chances*
- *Beyond Second Chances*
- *Another Chance – Peter's Story*

Cassie's Journey – A Life on the Run

Award-winning children's picture book:

Bluebirds in the Garden

Available at www.ritamboehm.com, www.Amazon.com, and some retail outlets.

In his own words:

On November 1st, 1942 we boarded a train at Fort Dix at approximately 10:30 for the port of embarkation. We arrived at the port in Staten Island at approximately 4 o'clock p.m. and at 2 p.m. November 2nd, we sailed for North Africa. The boat was the *John Ericsson,* formerly the *Kongsholm*, a Swedish liner.

JOHN ERICSSON

Length, overall	609' 0"	*Gross tons*	16,552	*Propulsion*	Diesel (2)
Beam	78' 0"	*Speed (knots)*	15	*Passengers*	5,461
Draft	29' 0"	*Radius (miles)*	13,000	*Cargo (cu. ft.)*	167,000

Built in 1928 by Blohm & Voss, Hamburg, Germany

Picture credit: https://history.army.mil/html/books/012/12-2/CMH_Pub_12-2.pdf, TROOPSHIPS OF WORLD WAR II BY ROLAND W CHARLES Naval Architect, copyright 1947

Note: *The John Ericsson, with its passenger load of close to 5,500 soldiers, was one ship among many in the large convoys heading to North Africa in November 1942.*

An Allied convoy, escorted by sea and air, near Casablanca, Morocco, in November 1942 on its way to take part in Operation Torch, the large British-American invasion of French North Africa

Picture credit: https://www.theatlantic.com/photo/2011/09/world-war-ii-the-north-african-campaign/100140/#img26

***

***Historical Background**: The naval battle for Casablanca, a major port city in what was then French Morocco, took place in early November 1942. Initially, Allied military leaders believed that they might be met by friendly troops and greeted as liberators. Instead, the Vichy French government (controlled by Germany) viewed the Allied invasion task force as hostile. A variety of naval engagements ensued, including attacks by German U-boats that resulted in the loss of four US troopships and at least 200 American soldiers. On November 11, Casablanca officially surrendered to the Allies. However, on November 15, a US cargo ship was torpedoed while approaching the city.*

These were the uncertain conditions under which Private Haight's ship docked in Casablanca on November 18, 1942.

The following are portions of a letter that Private Haight wrote to his mother from the ship and mailed from Casablanca.

He attempted to be upbeat, and, when viewed with the hindsight of present times and an awareness that two-and-a-half years would pass before he and the other soldiers headed home, his comment, "Don't worry because everything is alright and before you know it, I'll be home" is especially poignant. Also, as he would later learn, Dewey did not win the election.

Dear Mom:

This is just a short **note** *to let you know that at the present time I am somewhere in the Atlantic Ocean. We have been onboard for quite some time and all we know is that we are heading for a port somewhere in North Africa.*

The trip so far has been an uneventful trip. The weather has been very good most of the time, the days sunny and warm and the nights cool

[A section was cut out of the paper by the censors and then picks up as follows…]

Well, Mom, you can tell the family that your son is a good sailor, because I haven't been seasick once. I have taken to this trip like a duck takes to water.

All I can say at the present time is that I am well and in the pink of condition and looking forward to seeing land because the sooner we land, the sooner we will receive those welcome letters from home.

Well, Mom, I hope everything is going alright at home...I hope you and Irene are getting together during these dark days, but don't you worry because everything is alright and before you know it I'll be home.

Mom, drop me a line on how Irene is feeling. [His wife was 6 months pregnant at that time]. *Don't forget to tell the family to drop me a line because letters will be most welcome.*

Say, Mom, who won the football game on Election day? I understand that Dewey won the election...

Well, Mom, I'll sign off here with love and kisses and I'll write as soon as I land.

Love, Alty

The journal entries continue:

After 16 days of traveling on water, we first saw land on the 18th of November approximately at 9 o'clock. Our boat docked in the port of Casablanca in the afternoon, and we left the boat on the 20th at 2 p.m. for our location on the outskirts of Casablanca.

We stayed at this position five days and on the 25th moved to our gun position nearer the city of Casablanca and stayed until January 4th when we were ordered up to the front.

This postcard of prewar Casablanca was mailed by Private Haight to his wife, Irene. His message was blacked out by censors.

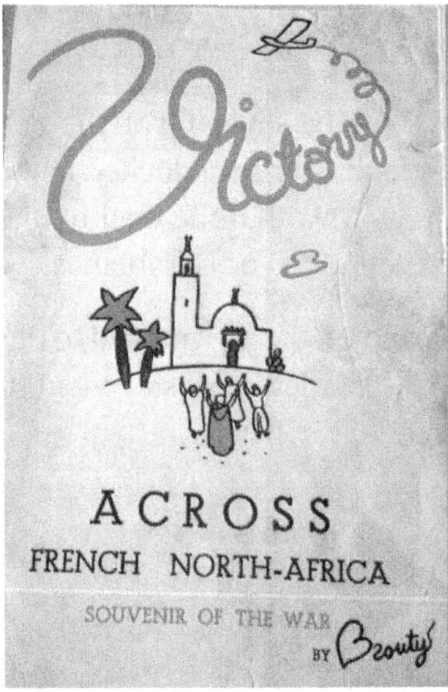

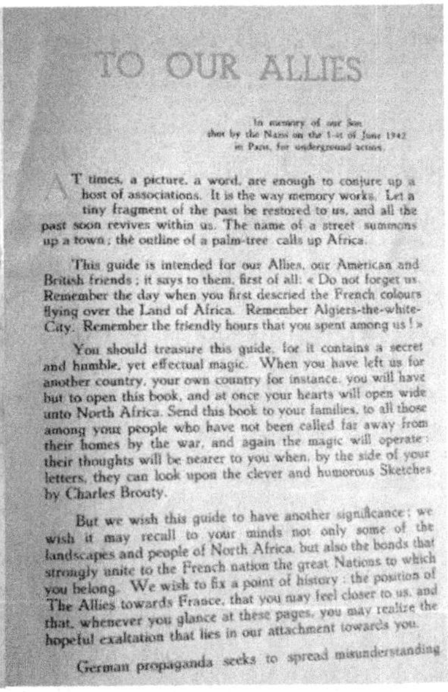

TO OUR ALLIES

In memory of our Son
shot by the Nazis on the 1-st of June 1942
in Paris, for underground action.

AT times, a picture, a word, are enough to conjure up a host of associations. It is the way memory works. Let a tiny fragment of the past be restored to us, and all the past soon revives within us. The name of a street summons up a town; the outline of a palm-tree calls up Africa.

This guide is intended for our Allies, our American and British friends; it says to them, first of all: « Do not forget us. Remember the day when you first descried the French colours flying over the Land of Africa. Remember Algiers-the-white-City. Remember the friendly hours that you spent among us ! »

You should treasure this guide, for it contains a secret and humble, yet effectual magic. When you have left us for another country, your own country for instance, you will have but to open this book, and at once your hearts will open wide unto North Africa. Send this book to your families, to all those among your people who have not been called far away from their homes by the war, and again the magic will operate: their thoughts will be nearer to you when, by the side of your letters, they can look upon the clever and humorous Sketches by Charles Brouty.

But we wish this guide to have another significance; we wish it may recall to your minds not only some of the landscapes and people of North Africa, but also the bonds that strongly unite to the French nation the great Nations to which you belong. We wish to fix a point of history: the position of The Allies towards France, that you may feel closer to us, and that, whenever you glance at these pages, you may realize the hopeful exaltation that lies in our attachment towards you.

German propaganda seeks to spread misunderstanding

Cover and page from a book from PFC Haight's collection of memorabilia. The 56-page book titled Victory Across French North Africa, Souvenir of the War *is a guide, with sketches and maps, to the various cities of French North Africa. The book was written by a Frenchman for "our Allies, our American and British friends." The first page includes a dedication "To Our Allies." Directly below the title are the words "in memory of our son shot by the Nazis on the 1st of June 1942 in Paris, for underground action."*

This small book appears to be a sort of olive branch from the Free French who opposed the Vichy government and fought alongside the Allied troops.

***

Historical background *– In June 1940, Chief of State Marshal Philippe Petain signed an armistice with Hitler within weeks after France was overrun by German soldiers. Petain then ran the government from Vichy and became a puppet of Hitler.*

Charles de Gaulle, working from London, objected to the legitimacy of the Vichy government and began working for the Free French movement.

Reference material:
https://www.smithsonianmag.com/history/vichy-government-france-world-war-ii-willingly-collaborated-nazis-180967160/

More letters:

Portions of a letter written on Thanksgiving, November 26, 1942. He suggests that next year will be different.

Dear Mom:

Well Mom, the situation is the same. We are still near the vicinity of Casablanca. We are pretty near settled now, but we have a lot of work in front of us...

Today is Thanksgiving Day, but it is just another day to us. I just can't stop thinking of that great big turkey you and the folks back home are eating. Whom are you spending the day with? Give everyone my regards.

I haven't received any mail as yet, we are expecting some next week. I hope you are feeling fine and that you are getting along alright...Christmas is almost on us. I guess it won't seem like Christmas this year, but don't you worry, we will make up for it next year...

Love, Alty

Portions of a letter dated December 5, 1942. He mentions delays in mail receipt, concerns about his pregnant wife, and the upcoming Christmas holiday.

Dear Mom:

This is just a short note to let you know I am still well and in the best of health. We are still located in the vicinity of Casablanca and it looks like we will be here for quite some time. That's about all I can say about our location here...

As yet we haven't received any mail and I guess you haven't received any up to this date. I know one thing, I'll feel much better once the mail starts coming...

Have you seen much of Irene? I hope so. I only hope she is well and that everything is alright...I guess Christmas this year will be a sad affair. Who are you going to spend the holiday with? Wish all the folks a Merry Christmas for me and tell Aunt Florence the sweater she made me is still coming in handy...

Love, Alty

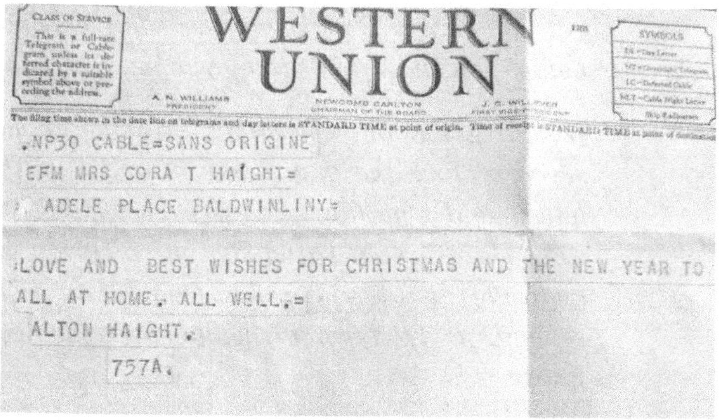

WESTERN UNION

.NP30 CABLE=SANS ORIGINE
EFM MRS CORA T HAIGHT=
ADELE PLACE BALDWINLINY=

LOVE AND BEST WISHES FOR CHRISTMAS AND THE NEW YEAR TO ALL AT HOME. ALL WELL.=
ALTON HAIGHT.
757A.

Christmas telegram saved by PFC Haight's mother

Portions of a letter to his mother written on Christmas day, December 25, 1942. Melancholy over his first Christmas away from family is reduced after receipt of long awaited mail from home.

Dear Mom:

Today it is Christmas here in North Africa and although there is not much Christmas spirit around us, we here at the camp are trying to make it a Merry Christmas day. We had our mess hall all decorated in Christmas style and even a Christmas tree. Our dinner was the best since arriving here. We had steak, sweet potatoes, peas, cake and candy and also beer.

This is one Christmas I'll never forget, yes Mom this is the first Christmas that the family didn't all get together, but Mom, don't let that get you down. Just keep your chin up and before you know it this thing will be over with.

We all got a big Christmas present. About seven o'clock the mail came in and I got 9 letters and a package, guess from who? Yes, Aunt Hazel...Aunt Hazel sent me a carton of cigarettes and a sewing kit. I now have four sewing kits. I got two on the boat from the Red Cross.

I also got three letters from Irene and she told me the big event should take place about the 2nd week in February...Irene said that she had pretty much near everything the baby would need, so I guess everybody has been doing all right for us. Thank them all for me. ...

Love, Alty

Back to the journal entries:

December 31, 1942

Casablanca, Morocco

Our first air raid. Our guns fired and we claimed one plane. This was one of the greatest thrills of my life.

Picture credit: https://www.ww2online.org/image/wrecked-german-aircraft-field-north-africa-probably-1942-43

1943

January 1943

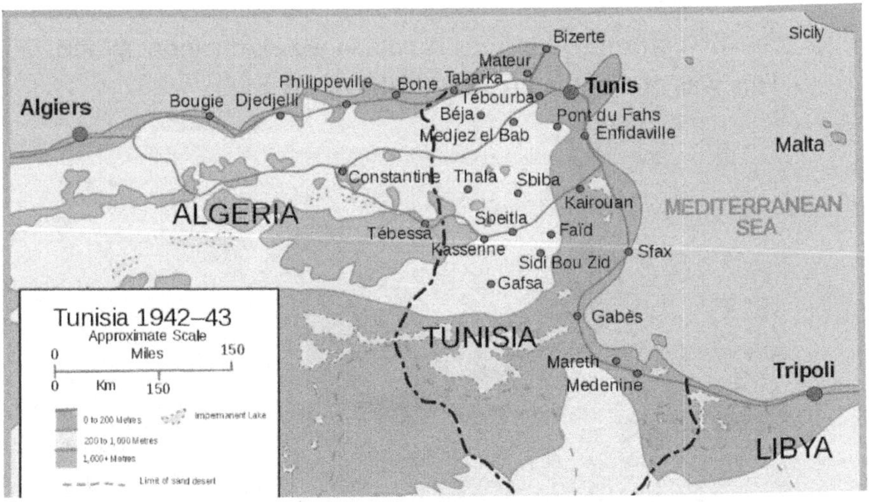

Map of some of the areas of engagement during the North African Campaign. Many of the places on this map are mentioned in the upcoming journal pages. Of particular interest is the area between Tebessa and Gafsa (in the middle of the map) where, in February, Allied troops engaged in a major battle with the Germans at Kasserine Pass.

Friday, January 1, 1943

Casablanca, Morocco

Restricted to area to await orders on our moving north. We all hoped the air raid would keep us there.

January 2

Still restricted and awaiting orders for move of over 1200 miles northeast to Constantine.

January 3

Today orders were finally received to start on our trip north. 68th took over our position and we began preparing for the trip.

January 4

At 6 a.m. we left Casablanca and headed north. 4 gun batteries and HQ. We were told we would be heading toward Constantine some 1200 miles away.

January 5

On the road. We traveled 250 miles yesterday and hope to cover same today. All traveling was done in the day. Weather good. Stop for the night in Oudjda, Morocco.

January 6 - Algeria

On the road. Today we went into Algeria. Stayed for the night at Sidi-bel-Addes in a large hall. All the boys got drunk. Weather was bad rain.

January 7

On the road today we hit the Atlas mountain range. We saw plenty of snow. Very cold and dry. Scenery beautiful.

January 8

On the road. Traveled a good distance today through mountain range. At nite we stopped for the week-end to rest and clean-up. We stopped in the heart of an orange grove in Blida.

One of the postcards saved by PFC Haight. Many were mounted in photo albums on brittle pages and became damaged over time. Removing the cards revealed that a small number of them had been mailed and contained messages to his wife, Irene.

January 9 - Blida, Algeria

In the orange grove. Today I shaved and washed – first time in 6 days. We saw our first group of English soldiers. So far since leaving Casablanca we have been eating C-rations and today we really filled up on oranges.

Postcard of a girls' school in Blida from PFC Haight's collection.

January 10 - Blida

In the orange grove. Our last day here. Tomorrow we hit the open road. All the trucks are now filled with oranges.

January 11- Setif

On the open road once again. Still in the mountains. Passed the outskirts of Algiers. Tonight we stopped at an English gas dump in Setif *[a city in Algeria]*.

January 12

We hit the open road early today and arrived in Constantine in early afternoon. This city setting in the mountains is one of most beautiful that I have seen so far.

Postcard of Constantine from PFC Haight's collection

January 13 - Constantine, Algeria

We camped here waiting for further orders. We camped on a race track and here we saw some very beautiful horses.

January 14 - Constantine

Today we got cleaned up once again. Took things easy and I plan on giving Constantine the once over tomorrow.

January 15 - Constantine

Visited the city but was very disappointed in it. Looks beautiful from a distance but not when you are close to it. Also had a bath and swim. I bathed in an outdoor pool in the heart of a large mountain. We ate in Constantine, but it was no good.

January 16 – Constantine

Today we had to get everything ready to leave tonight. This is our first black-out drive. We only have 100 miles to go.

January 17 - Tebessa, Algeria

We arrived here at 4 a.m. and it was raining. We stayed in the trucks waiting for daylight. At 10 o'clock we were ready for action.

January 18 - Tebessa

We were ordered to dig in and we figure we will be here some time, seeing that Tebessa is the main supply base and nearest to the front.

January 19 - Tebessa

Tebessa is a small town built within a wall.

Stone walls and the Arch of Caracalla, Tebessa, Algeria

Picture credit: https://commons.wikimedia.org/wiki/File:T%C3%A9bessa.4.jpg Free Media repository

January 20, 21 - Tebessa

This town is used as HQ for Americans, French, and English. There are also several hospitals and this is the receiving center for all prisoners. During our first week here, nothing happened. We took life easy. Then one JU-88 flew over our position but he was flying too high to fire. He was taking pictures of how strong Tebessa was protected.

JU-88 German World War II Luftwaffe twin-engine multirole combat aircraft
Picture credit: Wikipedia – Picasa

January 22 and 23 - Tebessa

This enemy soon became a regular visitor and he was known as Photo-Freddy. We tried to fire at him a number of times but they never came close. This JU-88 flew over or near our position every day taking pictures of different positions.

Portions of a letter dated January 22, 1943: He provides thoughts about his pregnant wife, hopes for mail from home, and assurances that he's healthy and doing fine.

Dear Mom,

...Things are about the same here. We are still living a real outdoor life. Today, it's very warm here somewhere in North Africa. This weather would be alright but at night we freeze and in the daytime we sweat.

I haven't received any mail yet, but I am looking anxiously forward to receiving some in the near future. I hope Mom by this time you have received some of my mail. I know receiving mail from me will help to make you feel better...

Have you seen Irene lately? Let me know how she is. Time is growing very short for the big event. How do you think you're going to feel being called grandmother? Got old fast, yes. I guess Irene has everything she needs for the baby now. How do the things look? Does everything meet with your approval? If they don't, let me know.

...Don't worry about me. I am in the best of health and feeling fine and looking forward to that day that I'll return to you and Irene.

Love, Alty

January 24 and January 25 - Tebessa

Other than this one plane, there was no action. However, with this enemy giving us a daily visit we expected enemy action. Here at this position we were taking life very easy and our living conditions were good.

January 26 through January 31 - Tebessa

Three of us (Van Wych, Butcher and myself) sleep in a large tent and almost every night we have a bull session until 10 o'clock. We were eating good. We bought eggs and chicken from the Arabs and almost every night we have some sort of snack. Some nights we had fried chicken or egg omelets.

The weather here was just about the same as we have had in other spots in North Africa. Plenty of rainy and cold weather. At night it was very cold with a heavy frost. Things here were going along very smoothly, then one day in the early afternoon, 5 planes came into the sky and went into a dive bombing effect trying to bomb the railroad. At first we all thought our position was being attacked. Where they dropped the bombs was only a mile from our position and the noise of the airplanes and bombs scared us.

German Ju-87 Stuka dive bomber

Picture credit: https://www.warhistoryonline.com/featured/amazing-facts-about-the-junkers-ju-87-stuka-it-had-a-top-speed-of-a-mere-255mph.html

February 1943

Tebessa, Algeria is on the upper left and slightly below and to the right is Feriana, from where an arrow points down to Gafsa.

These are the positions where PFC Haight and his fellow soldiers supported the Allied operations in their engagements with the Germans.

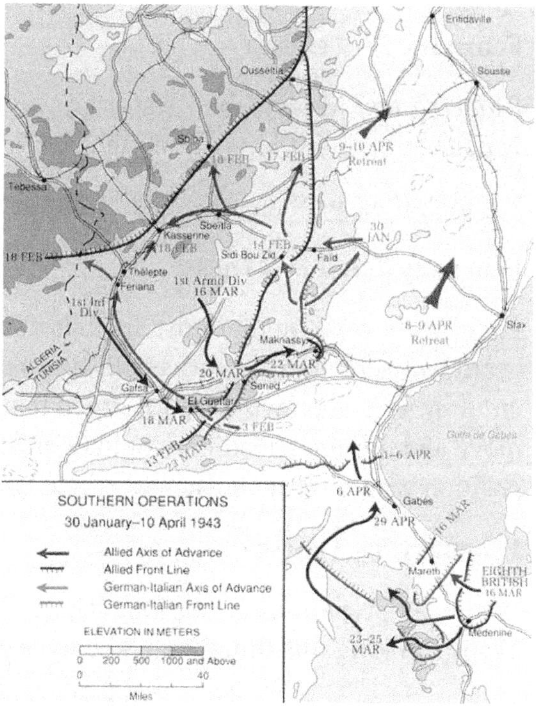

Picture credit: *https://history.army.mil/brochures/tunisia/tunisia.htm*

February 1 through 6 - Tebessa

Tebessa being attacked. Where they dropped their bombs was only a bit from our position and the noise of the airplanes and bombs scared us plenty. The enemy missed their target and no damage done. After this attack there were some high bombs dropped by a JU-88, but again they missed their target and no damage was done. After this excitement things once again settled down and we again started to take things easy. The news each day was getting better and the enemy was being pushed. So rumors started that we were soon to move close to the front.

February 2 - Tebessa

[Added later] My daughter Kathleen was born at 7:06 p.m. 7 ½ pounds. I didn't know it though.

We took it easy all day. No enemy action.

February 7 and 8 -Tebessa

For a while we thought it just another rumor like the rumor we heard we were going to move to Sfax [*a city in Tunisia, 450 miles away]*. Then we were informed that we were going to move and our new position would be near the front and our position would be at Gafsa.

February 9 - Tebessa

We began preparing for our long trip to Gafsa and we all were happy thinking this thing would be over within a month or so.

Note: *Two years later, Private Haight and many thousands of other Allied soldiers were still fighting in the midst of the European war theater.*

February 10 - Tebessa

Left at 6:00 p.m.

We were ordered today to move to Gafsa, a distance of 100 miles, moving at night. The weather was clear, but only a slight moon was out.

February 11 - Gafsa, Tunisia

Arrived here safely at 6:00 a.m. but we did damage one truck. It was a rough night for all. Battery set up on edge of desert.

We camped in an olive and palm grove. Met a group of Rangers for the first time.

February 12 - Gafsa

We fired today at enemy aircraft. Fired 178 rounds. Enemy driven off. Weather has been warm. Today we learned that we were front line troops and the enemy was 10 miles away.

Picture credit: Signal Corps
Part of a US Army anti-aircraft artillery crew manning a 9mm gun surrounded by gun shells and empty gun casings

February 13 - Gafsa

Today we had an old Arab doing our work. We're in the palm grove and we're living like kings, but the men up at the guns were having it tough living underground dirty and full of sand. Today we learned that the enemy was moving toward us. We were going to make a stand here.

February 14 - Gafsa

During the day it was quiet. At night the enemy out-flanked us and we were ordered to retreat in a hurry. We left equipment behind in this move. We left Gafsa at 10 p.m. We were one of the last to leave the city.

Historical Background: *On February 14, 1943, German General Erwin Rommel and his Afrika Korps launched an offensive against an Allied defensive line in Tunisia. The Battle of The Kasserine Pass was the United States' first major battle defeat of the war.*
https://www.history.com/this-day-in-history/battle-of-the-kasserine-pass

Postcard sent by PFC Haight to his wife Irene with the message "This is Gafsa, the place where Battery A made its retreat on February 14th. The place doesn't look like that now."

February 15 - Feriana, Tunisia

Arrived here from Gafsa at 4 a.m. At 10 a.m., we fired at enemy aircraft. Results not known. This stop is temporary. Waiting here for further orders. Weather cold.

February 16 - Feriana

Things are very quiet but we heard the enemy is still advancing. Gafsa fell to the enemy. Weather is still cold and we have been eating stew since Tebessa.

February 17 - Feriana

March order came at 4 a.m. By daybreak we were at Bou Chebka *[22 miles away]*. However we were ordered back to Feriana to be front line troops again.

***

Historical Background: *By the afternoon of February 17, Rommel's troops had occupied Feriana and Thelepte (roughly 24 km/15 mi southwest of Kasserine), forcing the evacuation, on the morning of February 18, of Thelepte airfield, which was the main air base in British First Army's southern sector.* *https://en.wikipedia.org/wiki/Tunisian_campaign#cite_note-51*

"On both flanks the Americans began to pull back to the Western Dorsal, evacuating Gafsa and Sbeïtla. On the night Gafsa was evacuated in rain and blackout over a narrow road choked, as an observer reported, 'bumper to bumper, from head to tail with tanks, artillery, infantry, French Legionnaires, camels, goats, sheep, Arab and French families with crying children, jackasses and horse-drawn carts,' an Ordnance detachment brought up the rear, pulling tanks and vehicles out of ditches. At Sbeïtla the last men to get out of town were two Ordnance officers who were firing the ammunition dump.

Rommel occupied Gafsa and Fériana and on 17 February overran Kasserine Pass in the Western Dorsal. He caused appalling losses in American men and equipment, but achieved no lasting victory. By 17 February the Americans had brought up the 9th and 34th Infantry Divisions from Oran and Casablanca, and the British had sent their 26th Armoured Brigade from northern Tunisia. After five days of hard fighting, Rommel was forced to withdraw to the coastal plain." *https://history.army.mil/books/wwii/Beachhd_Btlefrnt/ChapterVIII.htm*

February 18 - Bou Chebka

We set up at 6 p.m. Our mission here was to protect a field artillery outfit located in the mountains. All quiet and no evening action.

February 19 - Bou Chebka

Weather was good and we are once again settled down without enemy action.

February 20 – Bou Chebka

Weather good. At 11 o'clock I had a dizzy spell and almost fainted. An hour later aircraft were flying over our position. It was a full moon and planes were visible.

Our new position at Feriana was a suicide position. We stayed there 3 hours. In front of us was an airfield with gas and planes burning.

Picture credit: https://www.historynet.com

We were ordered back at 4 p.m. to Bou Chebka *[22 miles away]*.

February 21 - Bou Chebka

We all felt sure they were enemy planes. Later we were informed they were friends but we were scared last nite. Field artillery continues to blast all day.

February 22 - Bou Chebka

We were told today that the field artillery knocked out 2 German batteries yesterday. We were informed that field artillery was moving. We're good. No enemy action.

February 23 - Bou Chebka

March order came early and so did a big mail call. It was raining hard all day. We pulled out at 3 p.m. and the enemy advance patrol was only 4 miles away.

Soldiers at mail call.

Picture credit: https://www.nationalww2museum.org/war/articles/mail-call-letters-archives

February 24 - Tebessa

Moved back here for a rest period which we needed.

February 25 through 27 - Tebessa

The position that we occupied here was located about 5 miles away from our first position in this town. However we were about 8 miles away from the town. Our position was located in the foot of the group of mountains. The Guns section were placed out in the fields and rear group took up a position on the side of the mountains.

Soldiers from the 2nd Battalion of the 16th Infantry Regiment head east through Kasserine Pass on February 26, 1943, after Rommel's withdrawal.

Picture credit: http://liberationtrilogy.com/books/army-at-dawn/historical-photos/slideshow/

February 28 - Tebessa

Here we had plenty of trees. Here we were getting a much needed rest and taking life very easy. Every night we played cards in a closed van and we always returned for the night about 9 or 10 o'clock.

March 1943

March 1 - Tebessa

Heard today that I was a father – great news.
[Daughter Kathleen was born on February 2]

We were taking things easy all day. Weather good. No enemy action.

March 2-9

The weather was cold most days and of course we had plenty of rain and then we had our warm days. At this position we got a very good chance to clean up.

During our stay here we had no enemy action, although one day a JU 88 did fly over our position. Our guns did not fire.

Other than this there was no enemy action here. The food here was much better than we had been getting. Once again the rumors started that our time for moving was near. At first, we had no idea where we would move to. The news that came to us was improving each day and of course was better after receiving that set back *[at the Kasserine Pass]*. Finally we were told we were going to move and once again we began preparing for a move.

March 10 - Tebessa

March order came in the morning but we never pulled out until 6 p.m. Weather was good during the day, but rain started at night.

March 11 - Feriana

Arrived at night at 2 a.m. Our job here is to protect the largest airfield in Tunisia. English moved out and we took their place.

March 12 - Feriana

We had 6 German dive bombers over our position and airport. 2 hours later 6 more came. We fired 37 rounds and 5 enemy planes were knocked down. Bombs landed close to our position.

Picture credit: https://www.warhistoryonline.com/

March 13 - Feriana

Things were very quiet today. No enemy action. The weather was good.

March 14 - Feriana

Here we are still taking life easy and no enemy action. Weather good.

March 15 - Feriana

Today the enemy was over our position. An ME-109, but not for long because 2 Spitfires were on his tail. All three planes crashed about 5 miles from our position.

Weather good.

German Messerschmitt Me-109 fighter plane
Picture credit: https://www.historynet.com/one-oh-nine-messerschmitts-killing-machine.htm

March 16 - Feriana
Today it's raining. We were told today the American big push will start tomorrow. No enemy action today.

March 17 - Feriana

The big push started today. We took Gafsa in 30 minutes *[about 45 miles away]*. No enemy action here. Weather – raining.

March 18 - Feriana

We are all interested in the news waiting to hear of the big push. No enemy action here. Weather – raining and cold all day.

A picture titled "Tunisian Mud"
Picture credit:
https://cardboardwars.wordpress.com/2013/12/11/tunisian-weather-1942-43/

March 19 - Feriana

Weather good. No enemy action. Over 100 of our planes took off on bombing raids. Other than that, things were peaceful. Still taking things easy.

March 20 - Feriana

Weather - cold and cloudy. No enemy action. American aircraft very busy: B17, A-20, B-25, B-26 flew over our position. We are now making plans to move to new location at Gafsa.

American B-24s

Picture credit: https://warfarehistorynetwork.com/2017/06/30/the-boeing-b-17-flying-fortress-vs-the-consolidated-b-24-liberato

March 21 - Feriana

Weather good - warm. We heard today we were soon to move to Gafsa again. No enemy action. Our aircraft was again very busy.

March 22 - Feriana

Weather warm today. Our move to Gafsa was cancelled. No enemy action. Our aircraft was very busy. Over 100 planes and bombers flew over our position.

March 23 - Feriana

Weather warm. No enemy action. Our aircraft were again very busy. 5 complete flights flew over our position. All types of bombers and fighters were in this raid.

British Spitfires flying in formation over North Africa.

The pilot of one of these planes, W/Cdr Gleed, was shot down In April over Cape Bon and was buried at the military cemetery in Enfidaville, Tunisia.

Picture credit: *http://spitfiresite.com/2007/09/spitfires-over-gabes.html*

March 24 - Feriana

Weather warm. Heard today *[illegible]* crashed. No enemy action at our position. Our aircraft was again active flying over our position.

March 25 - Feriana

Weather warm. No enemy action. Our aircraft very busy and active. We expected an English general today but his visit was put off until tomorrow.

March 26 – Feriana

Visited by Major General Portiger of the English army. Killed our chicken today and ate her. No enemy action. Weather warm.

March 27 - Feriana

Weather warm. No enemy action. Our aircraft also wasn't active today. A very dull day.

March 28 - Feriana

Weather good. No enemy action. Things very quiet. Even our aircraft was quiet.

March 29 - Feriana

Weather cold and cloudy. No enemy action. A very quiet day for all concerned. Still no war news.

March 30 - Feriana

Weather cloudy and cold. No enemy action. A very dull day. Went for rations. Made our own supper – French toast.

March 31 – Feriana

Weather warm and cloudy. 2 ME 109's flew over our battery. We fired 8 shots. We claimed one plane. Our aircraft was also busy.

Downed German BF-109 aircraft

Picture credit: https://www.worldwarphotos.info/gallery/germany/aircrafts-2/bf_109/

April 1943

Feriana, April 1943
Picture credit: Panzernet.com

April 1 – Feriana, Tunisia

Weather cold and windy. No enemy action. Also, our aircraft were very quiet. Taking things easy as usual.

April 2 - Feriana

Weather cold and windy. No enemy action. Our aircraft busy again. Saw AP-5 for the first time today. Heard C Battery ran into trouble.

April 3 - Feriana

Weather warm. No enemy action. Pay day. Our aircraft busy again. Heard a battery was shelled by 88's wounding 12. Also today saw a new P-51 crash near our position killing the pilot. I didn't see the plane but was told about it. Today I was transferred to the Range section.

April 4 - Feriana

Weather good – warm. No enemy action. Our aircraft busy again. John Connelly and I moved to range section today. Captain R was in an accident, broken leg and arm.

April 5 - Feriana

Weather warm. At 1:10, six ME 109's attacked the airport dropping plenty of bombs. One bomb landed *[illegible]* yards from my tent. We fired our *[illegible]* gun. One A-20 hit, and several men at the airport, 2 serious.

American Douglas A-20 Havoc bomber attack aircraft

Picture credit: https://en.wikipedia.org/wiki/Douglas_A-20_Havoc

April 6 - Feriana

Weather very warm. No enemy action. Our aircraft very busy. In the morning an A-20 was blown up due to a faulty bomb. In p.m. we investigated a parachute jumper. It was one of our airmen.

April 7 - Feriana

Weather cold and windy. No enemy action. Our aircraft busy. Captain Harris, new BC *[Battalion Commander]* took command today. We saw another pilot make a parachute landing. A-20 made a belly landing.

April 8 - Feriana

Weather cold and windy. No enemy action. No action by our aircraft. From today on the airport we are protecting is now a bombing base. We fired our guns in calibration. Results good.

B-17 Flying Fortress bombers from the 414th Bombardment Squadron roll out on steel Marsden Matting in Tunisia, 1943. Public domain photo: https://ww2db.com/images/50b5a7a955e19.jpg

April 9 - Feriana

Weather cold and windy. No enemy or allied air activity today. Today we had our first real shower since leaving Constantine *[on January 16]*. Also prepared for an inspection.

April 10 - Feriana

Weather windy and slightly cold. Had an inspection by Col Henrick acting General of 2626 AA. No enemy or Allied action today.

PFC Haight and his fellow soldiers slept in pup tents much of the time.

This is a representative picture from 1943 of troops from Company F, 347th Infantry Regiment, 87th Infantry Division standing for inspection.

Signal Corps Photo: May 8, 1943
Picture credit: https://olive-drab.com/

April 11 - Feriana

Weather warm. No enemy action. Over 100 bombers flew over our position today mostly A-20's. Heard today 8th Army had taken Sfax *[Tunisian coastal city]* other than that, a very peaceful day.

April 12 - Feriana

Weather warm. No enemy action, although had one alert. Our aircraft were busy. Today we heard plenty of rumors. Heard Sousse *[Tunisian port city]* had fallen, but we don't know if it's true. Also rumored that we were to move soon.

April 13 - Feriana

Weather warm and a little rain in p.m. No enemy action. Visited airport today and looked over A-20's. We heard the taking of Sousse was true. We had our first meeting of our club and I was elected President. J. Van Wigalt, Vice President.

April 14 - Feriana

Weather cool and rainy. No enemy action or allied action. Saw our first movie since leaving the boat *[six months earlier]*. The picture, "The Devil and Miss Jones", with Jean Arthur was held at B-Btry.

April 15 - Feriana

Weather cool and cloudy. No enemy or allied action. Spent day having instructions. A very dull day. Heard Tunis was made an open city.

April 16 - Feriana

Weather cool. No enemy action. The air corps moved from airport. We saw a movie called, "Call Out the Marines". Late tonight we got orders to prepare for march order. Rumors we would move to Bone *[an Algerian seaport now called Annaba]*.

April 17 - Feriana

Weather warm. March order came and we left our position at 10 o'clock a.m. We traveled north. We passed through the city of Souk Ahras 130 miles from our start. We again went through Atlas mountain range. We stopped for the night at La Croix at 12 p.m.

April 18 - La Croix

[First] Wedding Anniversary

PFC Haight with wife Irene before leaving for North Africa.

Weather warm. We stayed here for the day, resting from our long ride. Orders came for us to move at night (11:30) for Beja.
La Croix is located in the mountains. Beautiful scenery.

April 19 – Beja, Tunisia

Weather HOT. Moved in here at 5:30. Our position is on top of a large hill. Here we are 30 miles from front and 65 miles from Bizerte and 70 from Tunis. Beja shows signs of heavy fighting and bombing.

British soldiers enter bombed-out town in Tunisia
Public domain photo https://commons.wikimedia.org/

April 20 - Beja

Weather warm. We were given prepare for march order at 8 a.m. and at 9:30 p.m. we were in new position in Hunts Valley. Hunts Valley was named after Major General Hunt of the British Army. In this valley, he let the German Army advance to within 75 yards of his position and then opened up with everything he had which was field pieces and small arms. German tanks were left ruined along the roadside.

Our moving into Hunts Valley is to protect Field Artillery and ground troops. It is claimed that when the actual advance starts, it will only take 4 days to have all of Africa in Allied hands. Our position in Hunts Valley is to protect left flank and we are located 7 miles from the actual front, and we are 30 miles from Bizerte and 35 miles from Tunis. We expect to move with the American Army as it moves. U.S. has replaced English soldiers at this point.

9th Infantry Field Artillery soldiers in action in Tunisia

Picture credit: https://9thinfantrydivision.net/

April 21 - Hunts Valley

Weather - rain. We expected big things at this position but the day was quiet! Many of our aircraft flew over. We saw German anti-aircraft fire at them. Field Artillery also heard.

April 22 - Hunts Valley

Weather warm. Quiet during the day and no enemy aircraft were seen. Tonight at 7:30, Field Artillery opened and continued all night. This may be the start of the big push.

April 23 - Hunts Valley

Weather warm. Field Artillery was very active. We could see these shells burst in the mountains. We also could see our own aircraft dive bomb enemy position. We had a night visitor. No action.

April 24 - Hunts Valley

Weather cool and rainy. Field Artillery very active. Two alerts in afternoon, but enemy planes were out of range. Our big drive starts tonight at 12 a.m. We expected action, being so close to thc front lines.

April 25, Easter Sunday - Hunts Valley

Weather warm. This morning we saw our infantry advance over the mountains. The day was very quiet. In afternoon, enemy planes were seen but were out of our range.

April 26 - Hunts Valley

Weather warm. We fired 2 rounds each at 2 ME-109's at 4 p.m. At 6 o'clock, march order was given. We pulled out at 8 p.m. At 11 p.m. one truck turned over a 15 foot embankment, injuring three.

44th AAA Brigade, Men of D Battery, 454th AAA Battalion, manning their gun in front of the Municipal Casino, Algiers

Picture credit: Coast Artillery Journal, *May-June 1948*

Note: *PFC Haight joined the 44th AAA Brigade later in the year.*

April 27 - Foot Hills – Near Front

Warm. After a very hard night, we arrived at our new position at 6 a.m. We dug in, but darn tired. We had several alerts and fired 2 rounds each at 4 Me-109s. One plane was seen falling.

April 28 - Foot Hills – Near Front

Warm. Today we saw plenty of air activity both sides. We fired 4 rounds per gun at 3 Me-109s. Through scope we could see aircraft bomb the enemy.

April 29 - Foot Hills – Near Front

Warm. We had several alerts today. At 4 p.m., Fw-198 flew over our position and we threw everything at him. He fell six miles up the road.

Fw-198
German Tactical reconnaissance light bomber
Picture credit: https://en.wikipedia.org/wiki/Focke-Wulf_Fw_189

April 30 - Foot Hills – Near Front

Windy. We were kept very busy today. We had our first alert at 4 a.m. and at 8 a.m., 23 Me's and an Fw dive bombed near us. We fired in the p.m. at 3 o'clock. 2 Me – 5 Rds. It was a tough day.

Picture credit:
https://www.onwar.com/wwii/chronology/194303.html

May 1943

Historical Background: *Late April through early May saw significant fighting in the northeastern corner of Tunisia into which the Axis forces had been driven. These forces still held Tunis and Bizerte. Operation Strike began on May 5. On May 7, troops from US 9th Division occupied Bizerte and 1st Armored Division reached Ferryville. The last Axis troops to surrender belonged to the Italian First Army, which surrendered on May 13th. In all, Allied forces captured 275,000 prisoners in Tunisia.*

Reference: Rickard, J (26 May 2017), Tunisian Campaign, November 1942-May 1943 *http://www.historyofwar.org/articles/campaign_tunisian.html*

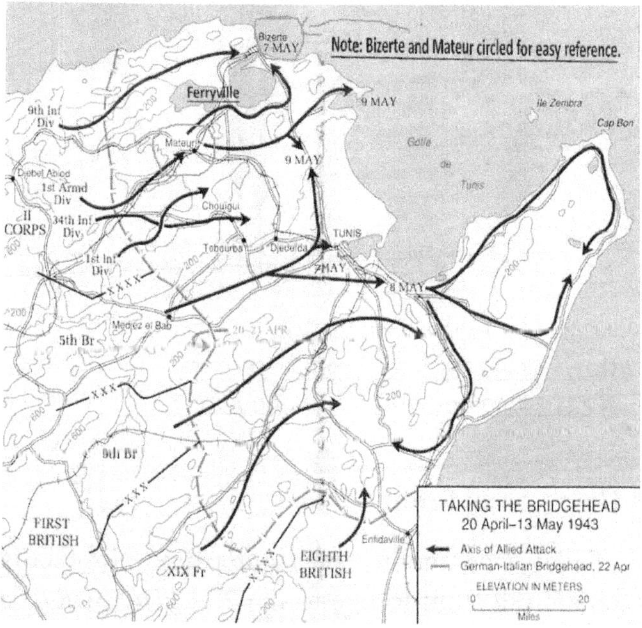

Picture credit: http://www.army.mil/cmh-pg/brochures/tunisia/p22-23(map).jpg

May 1 - Foot Hills - Near Front

Today we had two alerts, all in the morning. The enemy was always out of range. On the whole it was a very quiet day. Weather cool and rainy.

Our position here in the mountains is located 8 miles from Mateur and 20 miles North of Beja. The actual front is 5 miles away. Infantry battles can be seen at this position.

1st Armored Division M-4 tank heads for Mateur, Tunisia
Picture credit: https://www.med-dept.com/veterans-testimonies/veterans-testimony-anthony-s-dangelo

May 2 - Foot Hills - Near Front

Weather cool. Today was another very quiet day. No enemy action. I was transferred from Range to the 268 *[The SCR-268 Ground Radar was used by AAA batteries to provide height, direction and appropriate distance in front of enemy aircraft to aim the 90 mm gun].* Rumors on our returning home are getting very strong.

May 3 Foot Hills - Near Front

Weather cool. Today was even quieter than yesterday. No enemy action and no alerts. Heard we had advanced past Mateur and we have lost contact with the enemy.

May 4 - Foot Hills - Near Front

Today was another quiet day. No enemy action. At 5 p.m. march order came and at 6 p.m. we were on the road. We travelled 14 miles N to our new position. At 9 p.m. we were in our new position.

May 5 - West of Mateur Hill 609

Irene's Birthday.

Things were very quiet today and we were very close to the front lines. We heard D Battery was shelled. We found a vineyard near our position and we filled a 5 gallon water can with wine. The Germans were entrenched around this vineyard. The vineyard must have had 2000 gallons of wine.

May 6 - West of Mateur

This morning we saw several large flights of our aircraft. From our position we could see the German anti-aircraft fire on these planes. 1A – 2d was hit by German anti-aircraft. Finished the 5 gallons of wine today.

May 7 - West of Mateur

Rained all day. No enemy action. The day was quiet and a colonel inspected the Battery. Late tonight we heard that Bizerte had fallen to us and heavy fighting is going on in Tunis.

May 8 - West of Mateur

Today was another very quiet day. No enemy action. Bizerte was taken today by 2nd corps. Tunis by English 1st Army. Our march order to Ferryville was cancelled.

British troops advancing through Bizerte on May 8, 1943

Public domain photo: NA 2733 from the collections of the Imperial War Museums

May 9 - West of Mateur

Mother's Day. At 10 a.m. today we heard officially that the African Campaign had ended. "Unconditional Surrender." At 2 p.m. march order was given and at 4 p.m. we left our position for Ferryville. We arrived in Ferryville at 8 p.m.

Postcard sent from PFC Haight to his wife:

"Dear Irene, We passed through this town on the way up here to Ferryville. Note the wall around the city. All the towns and cities in this area are built with a wall, including Tunis and Bizerte."

May 10 – Ferryville *[directly across the lake from Bizerte]*

Weather warm. We set up our equipment today and we were ready for action. The day was very quiet. Our position is set on top of a large hill overlooking two large lakes one of which is the "Lake of Bizerte".

An aerial view of Bizerte, taken on May 10, 1943. After seven months of bombing, not a single building was habitable.

"'Bizerte was the most completely wrecked place I had ever seen,' Ernie Pyle reported. The town had been without running water for three months; typhus was present and cholera threatened."

Picture and text credit: http://liberationtrilogy.com/books/army-at-dawn/historical-photos/slideshow/

May 11 - Ferryville

The ground we are on is an old French military school The Germans were entrenched here. I walked along the beach. Bizerte is directly across from our position. We found 80 gallons of good wine.

May 12 - Ferryville

Weather warm. Spent a very quiet day resting and drinking wine all day. The weather has been warm but still too chilly to go swimming.

May 13 - Ferryville

Weather warm. Spent a quiet day. In the afternoon took a walk down to the beach and drank wine. Rumor started today that we are to make a 1500 mile trip.

May 14 - Ferryville

Weather warm. Spent a quiet day reading and resting. Took a walk around the area. At night I received 20 letters. 10 from Irene. 9 from mother.

May 15 - Ferryville

Weather warm. Another quiet day. Caught up on my corresponding. Heard today we could go swimming in the Mediterranean Sea. Also movies are open to us.

May 16 - Ferryville

Weather cool and windy. Received our campaign bar today. Rumors are that we are moving Tuesday. Tonight we saw the movie "Wake Island" and a live colored band.

May 17 - Ferryville

Weather cool and windy. Today we visited Bizerte. The city was completely ruined. We also went swimming in the Mediterranean Sea. Today the censorship on mail was lifted.

US Army tank in Bizerte
Picture credit: https://history.army.mil/brochures/tunisia/tunisia.htm

May 18 - Ferryville

Weather cool and windy. Went to Mateur today. Saw a movie, "Once upon a Honeymoon" with Ginger Rogers and Cary Grant. Censorship on mail lifted. Still talk of moving.

May 19 - Ferryville

Warm. A quiet morning. In the afternoon march order came at 1 P.M. At 3 we pulled to a bivouac area in Ferryville.

May 20 - Ferryville

Weather warm. Still in bivouac area. Today we started cleaning our equipment. Also a half hour infantry drill and we stand retreat. More wine.

May 21 - Ferryville

Warm. Went swimming again in the Mediterranean Sea in Bizerte. Had a hangover this morning. Had ham for dinner.

May 22 - Ferryville

A very quiet day. The rumors are we will move Tuesday to Oran *[coastal city in Algeria]*. Very warm.

May 23 - Ferryville

Weather warm. Was on guard *[duty]* all day. Missed a trip to Tunis. Things are very quiet. We hear no news.

May 24 - Ferryville

Very warm. Went to movies in morning, "A Yank on the Burma Road". Went swimming in the Mediterranean in the afternoon.

May 25 - Ferryville

Weather warm. Visited Tunis *[42 miles away]* and Carthage *[10 miles from Tunis]* on an all day visit. Saw truck and truckloads of German prisoners. Most of them young kids. Not much in Tunis.

Tunis, May 7, 1943

Cheering crowds line the square to welcome British soldiers.
Public domain photo from Australian War Memorial

May 26 - Ferryville

Weather cool and windy. Went to movies in morning. Spent quiet day in afternoon resting. I was worn out from the trip to Tunis.

May 27 - Ferryville

Weather cool. Went to a ballgame in afternoon. I was confined to the area for a week for missing retreat. We saw our first German air raid over Bizerte. Shrapnel fell in the battery area.

May 28 - Ferryville

Weather warm. A very quiet day. Spent the day in camp and nothing at all happened.

May 29 - Ferryville

Still in Bivouac area. We saw two air raids over Bizerte today. One in afternoon and one at night. I spent the day washing.

May 30 - Ferryville

Weather warm. Had Memorial Day services. Went swimming at Bizerte. Had fresh meat for supper – water buffalo. Went to local beach and English and Americans had a great night.

May 31 - Ferryville

March order came in morning and at 4 p.m we pulled out for Soliman – 80 miles away and east of Tunis. We are sent here to protect two English airfields.

June 1943

June 1 - Soliman

Soliman is located on the base of Cape Bon on the Gulf of Tunis and east of the city of Tunis. We are here protecting two newly constructed bomber airports.

June 2 - Soliman

Camped alongside of us are a group of South Sea Islanders from Tahiti. They are Free French and fought with the 8th Army. Went swimming today.

June 3 - Soliman

March order came today at 1 pm and at 7:30 we were heading for a new position 10 miles south of Enfidaville. We traveled blackout and the road rough.

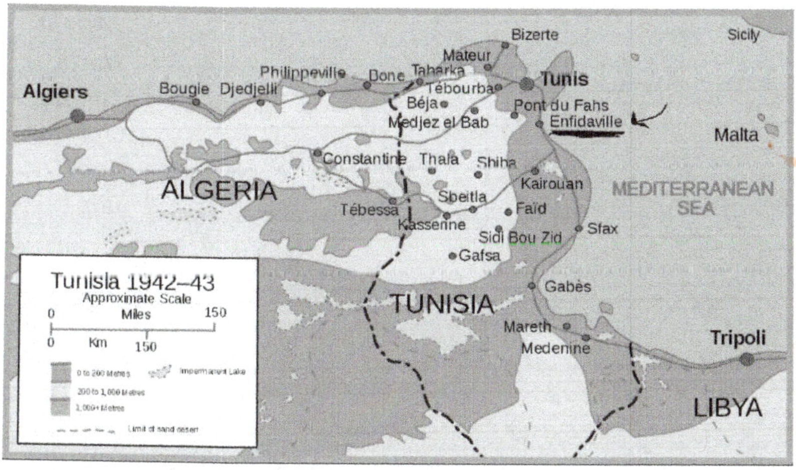

Map showing Enfidaville and the Mediterranean coast of Tunisia, which became the jumping-off point for the Allied invasion of Italy.

June 4 - Enfidaville

Our location is 10 miles south of Enfidaville and on the Gulf of Hammamet and 15 miles north of Sorisse. The airport has 300 B-25's. Went swimming in the Gulf.

June 5 - Enfidaville

Visited the airport and went through a B-25. Went swimming in the Gulf of Hammamet. Today we learned the 213th was back together again, all 3 battalions. Rumor has it we are to make a long trip from here in two or three days.

June 6 - Enfidaville

March order came at 1 p.m. and at 5:30 we were on the road. We traveled all night, mostly over dusty runs. We were heading for Cape Bon. *[127 miles]*

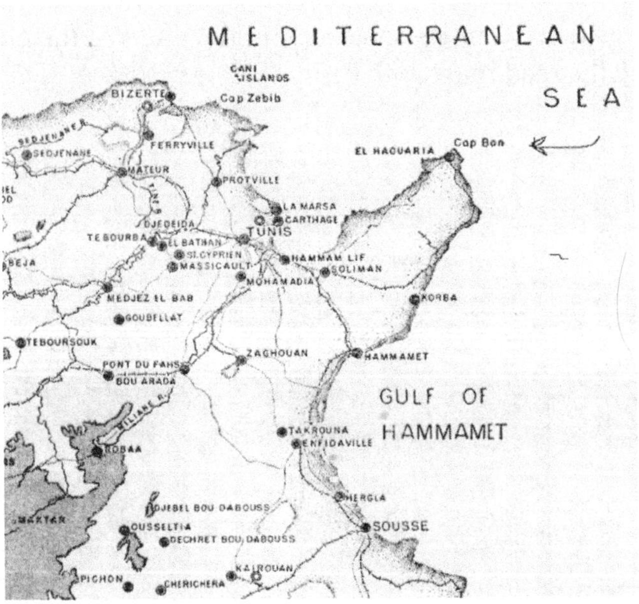

Map of North Tunisia showing Cape Bon

Picture credit:
https://www.ibiblio.org/hyperwar/AAF/II/AAF-II-6.html

June 7 - El Haouaria

We arrived at El Haouaria at 3 a.m. after a tough ride. El Haouaria is 4 miles from Cape Bon. Our position here is like "No Man's Land." Very barren. K.P. today

June 8 - El Haouaria

Today we had an alert for an hour while I was on duty on 268 [*SCR268 Ground Radar*]. Enemy planes were always out of our range. Other than that a very dull day.

SCR-268 Ground Radar, North Africa, 1943

Public domain photo: http://www.fortwiki.com/File:SCR-268A_Morocco_1943.jpg

June 9 - El Haouaria

Today was one of the dullest days I have had since arriving in Africa. It was warm and I read all day.

June 10 - El Haouaria

Went swimming at tip of Cape Bon. Explored an Italian ship full of German equipment which was half sunk off the coast. Also saw German 88's.

June 11 - El Haouaria

Weather was cool. Had a very quiet day. At night the Captain informed us that we had to receive basic training. Saw a movie called "The Hard Way" with Ida Lupino.

June 12 - El Haouaria

Today we explored the caves where the Germans and Italians hid before surrendering. The weather was cool.

June 13 - El Haouaria

My first year with the 213th. Went swimming at the Cape. Rumor has it that soon we are to take a long boat ride.

June 14 - El Haouaria

Starting infantry drill this morning. Went swimming in afternoon. Saw "The Pride of the Yankees" at the airport at night. Very warm tonight.

June 15 - El Haouaria

Had a very quiet day. I didn't feel very well. It was also cool and windy. At night, saw "Casablanca" and enjoyed it very much. Pay day.

June 16 El Haouaria

Today I recovered from a two day attack of dysentery. Had one glass of beer. A very quiet day.

June 17 - El Haouaria

Spent half the day reading and resting. In afternoon went on guard *[duty]*. Wind and sand is still blowing.

June 18 - El Haouaria

Finished my guard duty today. The wind and sand is still blowing. Saw a movie at night at the airport. "Private Harry Buckaroo" - the Andrews' sisters and Harry James.

June 19 - El Haouaria

Wind and sand still blowing. Rested most of the day. At night saw "Three Sons" at the airport.

Picture sent home by PFC Haight with inscription: "yours truly on Cape Bon. Summer 1943"

June 20 - El Haouaria

Our A.P.O. was changed from 668 to 758. Trips to Tunis started today. I expect to go Tuesday. The weather was fine today.

June 21 - El Haouaria

Today was a warm day and I spent the day resting and reading.

June 22 - El Haouaria

Went to Tunis for the day. Had a good time and drank beer. We left at 8 A.M. and got back at 9.

Postcard of prewar Tunis from PFC Haight's collection.

June 23 - El Haouaria

Spent a quiet day. Very warm day. Went on guard *[duty]* in afternoon. Helped set up new I.F.F on 268.

***Note**: "I.F.F. on 268" refers to setting up I.F.F. (Identify Friend or Foe) equipment on the SCR 268 ground radar. Ground radar for air defense first came into large-scale combat* *use in North Africa. Troops used the I.F.F. on the SCR 268 radar to determine whether aircraft belonged to Allied or German forces. Without this feature, there was a significantly greater risk of firing on friendly aircraft. This particular radar was used and appreciated by Coast Artillery units such as the one in which PFC Haight's served.*

Reference: The U.S. Army in World War II, The Technical Services, The Signal Corps: The Test, December 1941 – July 1943, George Raynor Thompson, Jan1, 1957, page 375

***

June 24 - El Haouaria

Another very quiet day. I finished my guard duty at 12. Still being troubled with dysentery. Don't feel any too well. Weather warm.

June 25 - El Haouaria

Learned today that we have a new battalion commander. Day was warm. I didn't feel well. At night saw the movie, "Maisie gets her Man" with Red Skelton and Ann Sothern.

June 26 - El Haouaria

Very hot day. Went swimming. Trips to Tunis cancelled. It's off-limits to all troops. Invasion should start soon. Saw a lot of action today. We had several alerts and we saw plenty of fireworks. We start packing our equipment Monday.

June 27 - El Haouaria

We learned the Germans hit one tanker during that raid last night. We also had an alert at 4 a.m. Went swimming and movies - "Northwest Rangers".

June 28 - El Haouaria

Today we were warned to be especially watchful for paratroopers. They are expected in this area. Very warm day. Rested most of day.

June 29 - El Haouaria

A quiet day and very warm. Went to the movies but it was called off because of a Red Alert which turned out to be nothing.

June 30 - El Haouaria

Today was a pay day. An American Red Cross worker (woman) gave us doughnuts. Our training period starts tomorrow.

The Red Cross Clubmobiles were staffed by Red Cross volunteers affectionately known as "donut dollies."

In addition to donuts, the Clubmobiles provided books, gum, coffee, cigarettes, and newspapers. Many had phonographs with loudspeakers playing popular music.

July 1943

July 1 - El Haouaria

Went swimming and the water is getting very warm. Today was our hottest day, seemed like it was over 100 degrees. Saw "White Cargo" - Hedy Lamarr.

July 2 - El Haouaria

Another quiet day. It was another very hot day. We were told General Eisenhower would visit our position but he didn't show up.

July 3 - El Haouaria

Was on a detail building a tank course. We were told we're now in 31st *[Anti Artillery]* Brigade and no longer with 2626. Went swimming. Water very rough. The weather was damp and seemed like a storm in the air.

Sherman M4A1 tank used by the British 8th Army in North Africa.

The M4 Sherman Tank was the most commonly used American tank in WWII. In addition to US and British troops, Free French, Chinese, and Soviet troops used these vehicles. The Ford Company produced more than 50,000 Sherman tanks from 1940 to 1945

Public domain photo: https://www.awm.gov.au/collection/C56076

July 4 - El Haouaria

Warm and hot. Went swimming and saw a movie, "The Battle of Britain."

July 5 - El Haouaria

Went to Tunis. Had pictures taken. Drank beer in English canteen and saw an English show. Very hot.

Photo sent to PFC Haight's wife Irene signed "Love, Alty" (left). Postcard sent to his wife (who was a registered nurse) with the message "Dear Irene, How would you like to work in this hospital? This town is located just the other side of Carthage (near Tunis). Love, Alty" (right).

July 6 - El Haouaria

A very hot day. On guard *[duty]* at 4 p.m. Prepared for tomorrow's inspection. Received Money Order today for $20.00, also did some typing for Rod Cullen.

July 7 - El Haouaria

Finished my guard duty. We had a big inspection today. Sent home money order. Very warm.

July 8 - El Haouaria

Two of our guns went out to the anti-tank range. Cullen and D--- went to Tunis for physical. I had a couple of hours of guard *[duty]*. Saw the picture, "Pittsburgh".

July 9 - El Haouaria

Slept all morning. In afternoon went out to the firing range. We saw an HE shell blast tanks. Today was windy and sandy.

July 10 - El Haouaria

Heard today that Sicily was invaded by American forces. The invasion started this morning. At night our forces were 12 miles inland. Other than that it was a quiet and peaceful day here. Wind is still blowing.

Picture of troops boarding LCI (Landing Craft Infantry) ships on July 6 in Bizerte, Tunisia, as part of the force of 3,200 landing craft and other vessels used in the invasion of Sicily. Bizerte served as one of the jumping-off points for the invasion. Thousands of troops left on LCIs for the trip across the Mediterranean.

PFC Haight's earlier journal entry indicating that he and his fellow soldiers might soon be taking a boat ride probably refers to rumors about their being part of this invasion force.

Picture Credit: National Archives Sc176486

July 11 - El Haouaria

Went swimming. Saw a movie, "Time to the Army."

The big news was Sicily. We were fighting on a 100 mile front and had taken 3 airports.

July 12 - El Haouaria

Went swimming in afternoon. Rested most of the day. Very warm.

July 13 - El Haouaria

A very hot day. Went on guard *[duty]* again today. Had classes in morning, rested in afternoon. No new news about Sicily.

July 14 - El Haouaria

Finished guard duty. A hot day. Missed a good show at airport. We have 10 towns in Sicily.

July 15 - El Haouaria

Weather warm. Went swimming. Saw a movie at airport called "In Old California" – no good.

July 16 - El Haouaria

My birthday. *[26 years old]*

Went to Tunis and had a very good day. Went with Johnny Prichard and Bud Pope. Saw *[movie]* "Orchestra Wives". Had ice cream and hamburgers.

Postcard of prewar Tunis sent by PFC Haight to his wife with the message on back, "Dear Irene, This is the entrance to the Arab section of Tunis and is right off the main section of Tunis. Love, Alty"

July 17 - El Haouaria

Another quiet day. Very hot. Went swimming. We had our usual Saturday inspection.

July 18 - El Haouaria

Went swimming and saw a movie, "Back Street". Very hot. We have been here six weeks. The longest time we have stayed *[in one place]* in Africa.

July 19 - El Haouaria

Weather very warm. Went on guard duty. Rested and read most of the day.

July 20 - El Haouaria

Finished guard duty. Another quiet day. At night we went on a hike from 8:30 p.m. to 10:30 p.m. Heard no news.

July 21 - El Haouaria

Went swimming and saw a movie at night. "The Road to Morocco" with Bob Hope and Bing Crosby. Very hot.

July 22 - El Haouaria

Had K.P. again. 2nd time in Africa. On K.P. you eat good. A very hot day.

July 23 - El Haouaria

Went to Tunis again with Johnny and Mike. It was a very hot day. We didn't do much but had a drink. Heard today that Palermo *[in Sicily]* was captured by Americans.

Public domain photo of bomb-damaged street in Palermo, Sicily. The Allies captured the city on July 22

July 24 - El Haouaria

We had our usual Saturday inspection. I was asleep during and got hell and an extra duty. It was very warm.

July 25 - El Haouaria

Today it was another hot day. It tried to rain. I read a book called the "Big Game". Swimming and movies were cancelled. Heard tonight at 11:45 that Mussolini resigned.

July 26 - El Haouaria

Another quiet day. Our big inspection cancelled till tomorrow. Rumors are going around that we are to move to Soliman in a couple of days for staging.

July 27 - El Haouaria

It rained today for the first time since April. Wind and sand was blowing hard. We also had our inspection. We were to fire, but cancelled. We also expect to move in a couple of days.

July 28 - El Haouaria

Today we got march order and started to take down the 268 *[Ground Radar]* at 7 p.m. We are to leave tomorrow before 9 p.m.

SCR 268 Radar
Picture credit: US Army photo from the Pacific War Online Encyclopedia © 2009-2011 by Kent G. Budge

July 29 - Grombalia

Today we started for our new position near Soliman at 7:30 a.m. We are to take over the 67 *[67th Coast Artillery Regiment]* position. We arrived at our new position at 11:30. 30 miles north of Tunis.

Note: *Grombalia was located at tip of Cape Bon not far from El Houraria. It was a military airfield used primarily by the US Army AF from June through October 1943 flying P-38 Lightnings and P-40 Warhawks.*

July 30 - Grombalia

Another hot day. Not much doing today. Rested up after the move. We had another inspection. One good thing, here we have a running shower.

July 31 - Grombalia

Very Hot. Visited the dentist. Had one tooth filled. Met Artie Dryer at Reg. Had some more melons today. Saw Mickey Rooney in “Yank at Eton”. I also received a package from Irene. We hear we are to move in a couple of days to a position 20 miles from Tunis. A B-17 base.

August 1943

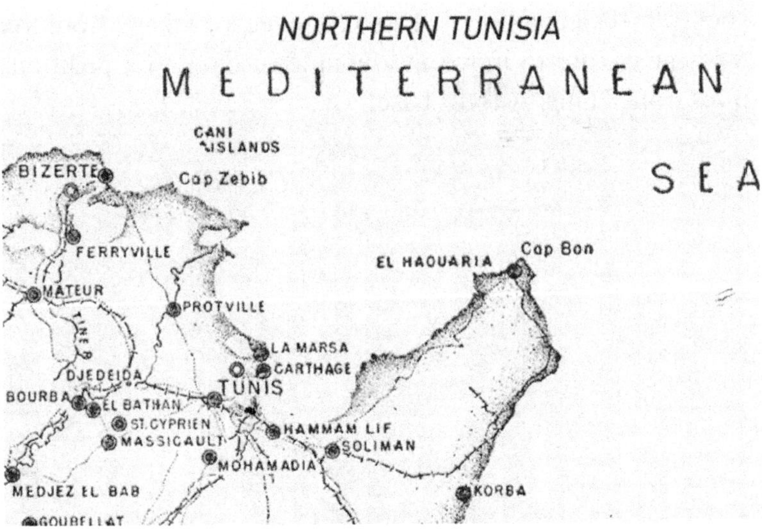

Map showing the part of northern Tunisia where PFC Haight was assigned. Grombalia Airfield was approximately 30 miles north of Tunis. The soldiers swam in the Mediterranean Sea at nearby Hamman Lif and Soliman.

August 1 - Grombalia

Very hot. Visited Tunis with Fred. Had two good meals. Saw a show. We hear we are to move Tuesday.

August 2 - Grombalia

Kathleen's sixth month birthday.

Another hot day. Rested most of the day. Went on guard *[duty]* at 4 p.m. Visited with 12 German prisoners last night. Had plenty of wine.

La Goulette, the port of Tunis, saw significant Allied and Axis bombing activity and would not have looked like this in August 1943 when PFC Haight was in Tunis.

Picture credit: Postcard of prewar port of La Goulette, the port of Tunis, from PFC Haight's collection.

August 3 - Grombalia

Today I hitch-hiked to Mateur 100 miles from here to see Bob Howell *[a friend from home]*. I got there at 2 p.m, left at 6 and was back at 12. A very hot day.

August 4 - Grombalia

Today I rested most of the day. I was plenty tired after that long trip. It took 15 hours in all. Another hot day. Had another cold shower.

August 5 - Grombalia

Went swimming again today at our old location at Soliman as usual, another hot day.

August 6 - Grombalia

Rested most of the day. We had 4 watermelons and all the grapes we want. Another hot day.

August 7 - Grombalia

Visited Tunis again today. We had our pictures taken and saw two shows. One was given by the English E.N.S.A. Very good. *[ENSA is the acronym for the Entertainments National Service Association, an organization set up to provide entertainment for British troops during WWII.]*

Postcard of prewar Tunis sent by PFC Haight to his wife with a message on the back reading "Dear Irene, This is a famous palace in Tunis. It's quite a beautiful building. Love, Alty."

August 8 - Grombalia

Spent today playing bridge all day. Just another quiet day around here.

August 9 - Grombalia

A nice cool day here. Not much doing. Our P-38 base across the street was very active today. Went on guard duty.

American Lockheed P-38. More than 10,000 P-38s were manufactured during WWII.

Picture credit: https://www.military.com/daily-news-

August 10 - Grombalia

Took things easy today after coming off guard duty. Today was windy and cool.

August 11 - Grombalia

Went swimming at Soliman. Saw a movie at the airport. Another hot day.

August 12 - Grombalia

Today another real hot day. Rested most of the day. Saw Bob Hope and Frances Langford at the airport.

Bob Hope entertaining WWII troops

Picture credit: https://www.nationalww2museum.org/

August 13 - Grombalia

Yesterday Old Man Walter Rye left us. He started for home. Saw a movie at the airport. Very warm.

August 14 - Grombalia

Another quiet and warm day. Had our Saturday inspection. Rested most of day.

August 15 - Grombalia

Today we had ice cream for dinner. Went swimming. Heard today I was going to be transferred to 31st Brigade.

August - 16 Grombalia

Went on guard *[duty]* today at 4 p.m. Rested most of the day. Another very hot day. Saw a P-38 crash nearby. No one hurt.

Downed P-38

Picture credit: https://www.worldwarphotos.info/gallery/usa/aircrafts-2-3/p-38-lightning/lockheed-p-38-lightning-crash/

August 17 - Grombalia

Went swimming today at a new beach. Plenty of people on it. Had ice cream. Very hot. We were swimming at Hamman-Lif.

Heard Sicily fell today.

August 18 - Grombalia

A very hot day. Saw a movie at the B-38 base across the street. Also went swimming.

August 19 – Grombalia

Went to Tunis and saw 3 movies.

At 8:30 p.m. Lt. Bethany met me at the Red Cross and told me I was transferred and was to leave tonight.

August 20 - On the Train

We pulled out at 2 a.m. 19 of us in one freight car. We were heading for Algiers. We crossed the Tunisia, Algeria border at 4 p.m.

August 21 - On the Train

We are traveling slow but sure. Made $15.00 selling to the Arabs. Stopped outside of Constantine for several hours. So far on the trip we were eating good. Plenty of eggs and melons. Selling clothing, I made $15.00

August 22 - On the train

We stayed in Krubo 14 hours. We traveled good until we hit Setif. Here we saw 15,000 German and Italian prisoners going to Algiers.

German and Italian prisoners of war at the Grombalia POW camp

Public domain photo:
https://en.wikipedia.org/wiki/Tunisian_campaign#/media/File:Gromalia_prisoner_of_war_camp.jpg

August 23 - On the train

We left Setif at 4:30 this morning. Once again we were traveling good. Passed thru the Atlas Mountains again. We arrived 6 miles outside of Algiers. We spent the night here.

August 24 - Algiers

We arrived here at 9:30 after losing our group. The 209th C.A.A.A *[Coast Artillery Anti-Aircraft]* picked us up at 1 p.m. We were given a new A.P.O 512 and address 6675 GOR. Also drank wine nearby

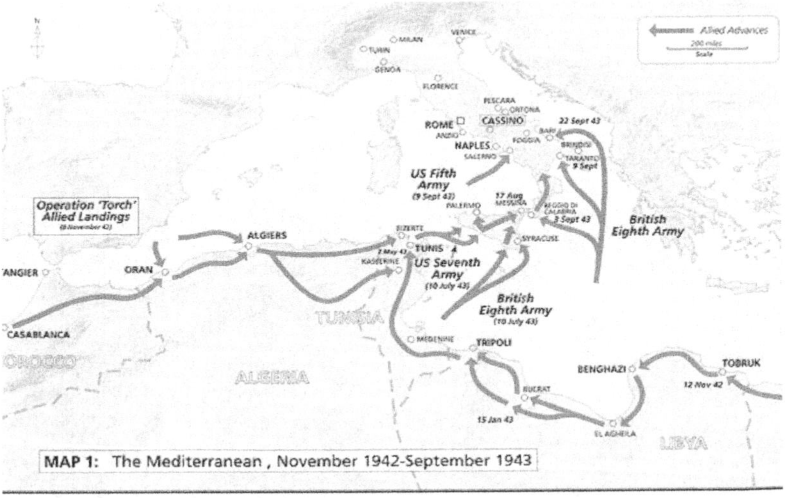

MAP 1: The Mediterranean , November 1942-September 1943

Map showing Algiers, Algeria, in relationship to Bizerte and Tunis, Tunisia, and the invasion of Italy.

Picture credit: https://www.matthewparker.co.uk/books/Map1-The-Mediterranean-November-1942-September-1943.html

August 25 - Algiers

Today I was interviewed and assigned to the supply room. So far I like the change. The work looks swell.

August 26 - Algiers

Today I took over complete control of the supply room. So far everything is swell, neat and set up. 209th got march orders today. Saw a movie.

August 27 - Algiers

Today we got march order and at 6 p.m. we moved over to the 74th A.A. attached to Btry A. Here we moved into barracks.

August 28 - Algiers

We all worked laying floors and making beds for the barracks. We are now located 3 miles away from Algiers. Had some beer today.

August 29 - Algiers

Today I was busy with supply records. I heard that there was no rating for supply. At night took a walk into town.

Algerian War Memorial, Algiers 1943
Picture credit: https://www.awm.gov.au/collection/C336784

August 30 - Algiers

Worked all day on records. At night went into Algiers on pass. Had some good wine and food. Mostly walked around seeing the city.

August 31 - Algiers

Took things a little easy today but was busy most of the day. At night saw a movie at the *[illegible]* located across the street.

September 1943

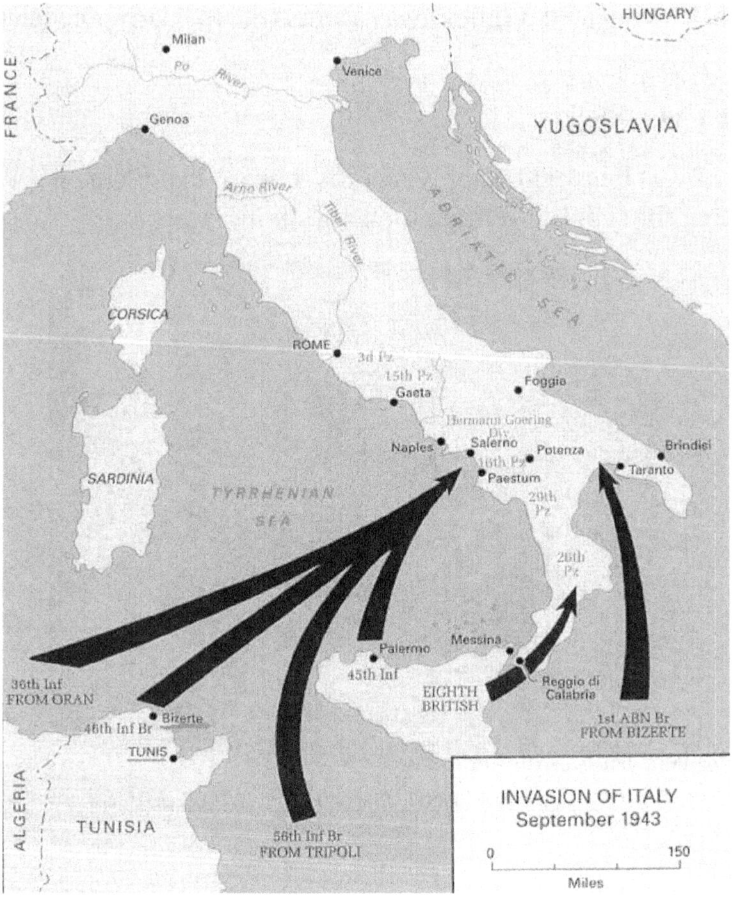

Map shows the importance of North Africa to the invasion of Italy on September 3rd, 1943.

48th infantry sailed from Bizerte, Tunisia. The 38th Infantry sailed from Oran, Algeria.

Picture credit: US Army Center of Military History

September 1 - Algiers

Today I went to the Regimental Supply Officer for schooling in supply and to set up books. At night saw a movie. “Time to Kill”.

September 2 - Algiers

Spent another day learning about supplies. Tonight I drove a 2 ½ ton truck around Algiers for the first time. Saw a movie, “The Woman of the Year”.

September 3 - Algiers

Heard this morning that Italy was invaded. Spent the day going out to the 1st guard depot getting supplies. Saw a movie at night.

September 4 - Algiers

Yesterday I received clothing and spent the day issuing that. At last I got a pair of cottons. At night I had a few drinks and a meal at a bar nearby.

September 5 - Algiers

Had a couple of sore feet today so tried to take it easy. They had me going in the morning, but I managed to rest in the afternoon.

September 6 - Algiers

Another busy day with supplies. Went out to the depot in the afternoon. At night saw a movie called, “I Follow the Band.”

September 7 - Algiers

Made two trips today out to the first General Depot. At night, went and had plenty to drink, mostly beer.

September 8 - Algiers

Once again busy with supplies. Went out to 1st General Depot twice. Took it easy at night.

September 9 - Algiers

Today drove a weapons carrier for first time out to 1st General. The weather has been very warm.

Dodge half-ton weapons carrier used in WWII before being replaced by the three-quarter-ton truck.

Dodge was the sole producer of the latter for the US Army, building more than 255,000 units from April 1942 to August 1945.
Picture credit: Alf van Beem - Own work, CC0, https://commons.wikimedia.org/w/index.php?curid=45894149

September 10 - Algiers

Spent most of the day getting wood for the boys. No movies so went to bed early.

September 11 - Algiers

Made a trip to 1st General, also to the St. George Hotel (the home of the Generals). *[The Allied Force Headquarters (AFHQ) was located at the St. Georges Hotel]*.Had a shower at the Red Cross. At night went to movies at the M.P's.

General Dwight Eisenhower and Prime Minister Winston Churchill in Algiers in 1943.

Picture credit: https://www.awm.gov.au/collection/C361812

September 12 - Algiers

Just another busy day. Twice out to the Depot. At night saw a movie at the M.P. A very warm day.

September 13 - Algiers

Once again made two trips to the General Depot. It was another very hot day. At night went to the movies at the signal corps.

September 14 - Algiers

Not much doing with supplies today. I took off for Algiers at 7:30 and spent the day window shopping. Had a lovely meal. Saw a movie.

September 15 - Algiers

Spent another busy day at the Depot. It also rained today. Saw a movie at night between the rain drops.

September 16 - Algiers

Today we got orders to move. Spent a busy day packing. We were only going three miles to the 74th Regimental Hqrs. We moved in at three.

September 17 - Algiers

Today we spent the day getting settled. Once again we are living in tents, but big tents. The rain finally stopped today.

A tent city in North Africa with city in background. The sign reads "Military/no trespassing"

Picture credit
https://www.ww2online.org/image/small-picture-tent-city-north-africa-august-1943

September 18 - Algiers

We have moved here to get equipped. We expect to stay here two weeks. The weather is still very warm and they still have me plenty busy.

September 19 - Algiers

Today took it a little easy. Took a ride with my supply officer. Our commanding officer is *[illegible]* to get tonight. Saw "Casablanca" again.

September 20 – Algiers

Today I went on guard *[duty]*. Our Major is no longer the swell guy we thought he was. We are all about ready to give up.

September 21 - Algiers

Today I came off guard *[duty]* and heard that we would move in about 7 to 10 days. We also got our new shipping number.

September 22 - Algiers

Today was one of those bad days. The Major was hounding me and everyone. We had a showdown inspection.

September 23 - Algiers

Spent another day working on supplies, but it seems I just can't please this Major. Took a ride in a jeep this afternoon.

September 24 - Algiers

Conditions were a little better this afternoon. Still no passes. Took a shower at the Red Cross.

September 25 - Algiers

Things were just about the same today. Stayed in the Supply Room to stay away from the Major.

September 26 - Algiers

This was just another working day. The Major made me walk 5 miles to church at El Biar *[a suburb of Algiers]*. The weather is getting cool.

September 27 - Algiers

Spent the day making out requisitions to draw our final equipment before we move.

September 28 - Algiers

Today it was raining cats and dogs most of the day and darn cold. Stayed inside working on supply records.

September 29 - Algiers

Still cold and still raining. Went out to the depot to draw our equipment.

September 30 - Algiers

Today was pay day. Also the rain finally stopped. Rumor has it we move Sunday or Monday. Saw a movie, "China Bird".

Algerian 5 Franc note found with PFC Haight's memorabilia

October 1943

October 1 - Algiers

Nothing much happened today except that we drew clothes at the Depot and my supply officer leaves them there.

October 2 - Algiers

Spent the whole day fixing the mess my Lt got me into. Had a shower at the Red Cross and saw the movie, "Time to Kill" for the second time.

October 3 - Algiers

Today we prepared for our long awaited march order. Although everything is packed, we don't expect to move until Tuesday.

October 4 - Algiers

Spent the whole day packing the trucks. We leave for Bone at 7:30 Tuesday. At night, Hank and I had 3 bottles of wine.

October 5 - Algiers

We left El Biar at 7:30 and also the Major went ahead. We traveled 200 miles and stayed at Setif. We saw a movie here. Also had some wine.

October 6 - Setif

We left here at 7 a.m. We had a tough nite. It rained and it rained late today. We arrived in Bone at 5 p.m. *[Bone is a seaport city in the northeastern corner* of *Algeria, close to Tunisia]*.

Picture credit: May-August 2002 Issue of Field Artillery Journal, *Robert C. Baldridge*

October 7 - Bone

We are bivouacking with a QM *[Quartermaster]* outfit just two miles outside of town. We didn't do much today but rest up after our trip.

October 8 - Bone

Today we started to move our equipment down to the GOR Room *[Gun Operations Room]* here in Bone. At night, Hank and I visited the bars in Bone.

October 9 - Bone

Today we moved into the GOR. Room which is located in a school house. The Major hasn't changed any. Still as lousy as ever.

October 10 - Bone

Today I went with my beloved friend the Major, to the quartermaster to get kitchen equipment. We are setting up our own kitchen tomorrow

October 11 - Bone

This morning, the Major and I had a good fight. In the afternoon I was relieved of my duties in the supply room and made a plotter.

Note: *Plotters were responsible for plotting Allied and enemy aircraft positions.*

Representative pre-WWII picture of a plotting table in a US Coast Artillery plotting room.

Public domain photo:
https://en.wikipedia.org/wiki/Plotting_room#/

October 12 - Bone

Today I had my first crack at plotting. I am not too crazy about it. At night, Hank and I bought a bottle of Scotch from the English *[for]* 400 Fr.

October 13 - Bone

I started this day working from 12 a.m. to 8. Slept most of the day cause it was raining.

October 14 - Bone

Today worked from 8 a.m. to 4 p.m. I didn't do any plotting. Just sat around and read. At night the English put on a stage show. Very good.

October 15 - Bone

Not much doing today. Took a shower in the morning and worked from 4 p.m. to 12 a.m.

October 16 - Bone

Today was on K.P. and it was the toughest K.P. that I have ever put in. The Major keeps you stepping. Went on duty at 12 a.m.

October 17 - Bone

Came off duty at 8 a.m. Went to an English church service. Rested most of the day. I plotted two missions in the G-O-R. Room.

Cathedral school in Bone, Algeria
Picture Credit: http://annaba.net.free.fr/html/bone.lycee.htm

October 18 - Bone

Went on duty at 8 a.m. Came off at 4 p.m. Spent a very quiet day. Hank and I are still missing our bottle of Scotch.

October 19 - Bone

On today from 4 to 12. We had a mission at 10 p.m. Slept most of the day.

October 20 - Bone

On duty from 12 to 8 and I plotted 2 missions before 12. Played Ping Pong all afternoon.

October 21 -Bone

Went on pass today. Saw a movie "Tall, Dark and Handsome". Nothing to this city. Had something to eat at the English canteen.

October 22 - Bone

Today we had another inspection. General Tobin of 44th Brigade was here. Was on duty from 8 to 4.

October 23 - Bone

Mother's birthday.

This was a very quiet day. Played Ping Pong most of the day. General Tobin believes we will be back in Algiers in 2 weeks. We had a rifle inspection this morning. On duty from 4 to 12.

October 24 - Bone

I was on fatigue duty but had very little to do. Rested most of the day. Didn't feel any too good.

October 25 -Bone

Today was my day off. I went into Bone again. Saw a movie "Two Yanks in Trinidad".

Bought a gift for Irene. It was a sunny day.

View of a street in Bone Algeria, 1943

Picture credit: *https://www.awm.gov.au/collection/C331072*

October 26 -Bone

Worked from 8 to 4. Didn't do very much but rest. Weather has been like early fall back home.

October 27 - Bone

Today had my first schooling on the 50 cal machine gun. Worked from 4 to 12.

October 28 - Bone

At school again today on the 50 cal machine gun. Rested on my time off. Worked from 12 to 8.

American soldiers operating a 50-caliber machine gun, 1944

Picture credit: https://www.ww2online.org/image/mounted-50-cal-browning-machine-gun-cassino-italy

October 29 - Bone

This was my day off but had to go to school. In the morning went to town. Had a steak which was like rubber.

October 30 - Bone

Was on duty in the Room from 8 to 4. Heard today we would move Tuesday to Philippeville and be with 44th Brigade.

October 31 - Bone

Was on duty from 4 to 8. Today was pay day. It was a very quiet day for me.

November 1943

November 1 - Bone

Today I was on K.P. and it was very much easier this time. Playing around at night, I sprained my ankle.

November 2 - Bone

March orders came today and we pulled out of Bone at 1 p.m. We arrived at Philippeville – 60 miles away – at 4 p.m. at the 44th Brigade area.

November 3 - Philippeville

We are set up with the 44th Brigade. Went to the hospital and had an x-ray taken of my foot – nothing broken.

Note: *Philippeville is a port city in Algeria. A city, like Bone, where the Allies brought in tanker ships of fuel which was stored at tank farms and distributed through an extensive pipe line constructed to support the Allied airfields in eastern Algeria.*

November 4 -Philippeville

Spent a very quiet day. Rested in the morning. In the afternoon had a lecture on the M1 Rifle. Rain stopped the talk.

November 5 - Philippeville

It rained all day. So most of the day was spent in my pup tent. The rain continued all day and night.

November 6 - Saturday, Philippeville

The rain stopped in the morning, but right after lunch it started again and continued all day and night. In the afternoon we put up big tents for those forced out of their pup tents.

Signal Corps Photo: May, 1943
Representative photos of soldiers living in pup tents and enduring rainy conditions.

November 7 - Philippeville

It rained for half the morning and then on and off all day. Today we made beds for the big tents in which we will sleep.

November 8 - Philippeville

Went on pass today and did a lot of shopping. Had a pretty good time but little to drink. It rained in the morning.

November 9 - Philippeville

Today I had a warm shower. I was on guard *[duty]* for 4 hours. It rained all night.

November 10 - Philippeville

Was sick today with the chills and fever and spent the day in bed. It rained all day and night.

November 11 - Philippeville

It didn't rain in the morning but it did in the afternoon. Helped with the issuing of clothing.

November 12 - Philippeville

Today we moved from this mud hole to a hotel on the other side of town over-looking the Med Sea.

Postcard of prewar Philippeville from PFC Haight's collection. Neither the city nor the hotel would have looked like this when he saw them.

November 13 - Philippeville

We spent the whole day cleaning up the hotel and finished moving our stuff from the bivouac area.

November 14 - Philippeville

Today was a beautiful sun shining day. Didn't do much for the day, but at night had a blue fish dinner. Real good.

November 15 - Philippeville

Wasn't feeling too good today. Had an upset stomach so spent most of day resting.

November 16 - Philippeville

Still feeling bad so once again spent most of my time inside and in bed.

November 17 - Philippeville

We took a nice long hike up the mountainside. Other than that rested most of the day.

November 18 - Philippeville

Went to town today. Saw 2 movies, "Holiday Inn" and "Silver Skates". In between movies went window shopping.

November 19 - Philippeville

Still being bothered by stomach aches. Went on a hike but had to drop out. Rested most of the day.

November 20 - Philippeville

Had a rifle and room inspection this morning. The General also inspected. Other than that it was a very quiet day.

WWII soldier with the standard issue M-1 carbine rifle similar to the rifle that would have been the subject of the rifle inspection.

Picture credit: quora.com/the-wwii-30-M-1=carbine.jpg

November 21 - Philippeville

This being Sunday, was a day of rest and I took full advantage of it. Reading and resting all day.

November 22 - Philippeville

Today I went to town on pass. Saw two movies, "Me and My Gal" and "A Shadow of a Doubt". In morning went on a hike.

Postcard of prewar Philippeville from PFC Haight's collection

November 23 -Philippeville

This morning we took another hike and in afternoon had our lesson. It was cold and raining most of the day.

November 24 - Philippeville

This morning we had our usual hike and class in the afternoon.

November 25 - Philippeville

Rested most of the day. Had a class in morning and one in afternoon. Weather is cold and damp.

November 26 - Philippeville

Had our three mile hike this morning. Afternoon we had off to prepare for inspection.

November 27 - Philippeville

Today we had a general inspection. General Tobin also inspected. We had the afternoon off.

November 28 - Philippeville

Today was a very dull day. Spent the whole day inside reading. It was cold and damp.

November 29 - Philippeville

Today went to town on pass and saw two movies, "Zeigfield Girl" and "Pittsburgh". Had tea at the canteen.

November 30 - Philippeville

Today was another dull day. Had those classes all day and very boring.

Representative picture of WWII soldiers attending a class.
Picture credit: *https://www.ww2online.org/*

December 1943

December 1 - Philippeville

Went to town on pass. Saw "Zeigfreid Girl" over. At night visited an Italian family.

December 2 - Philippeville

Today it was cold and damp. Had a class most of the day. Received lots of Christmas presents today.

December 3 - Philippeville

We had our morning hike and class in afternoon. The weather was nice and warm today.

December 4 - Philippeville

Had our inspection in morning. In afternoon drank and ate in nearby restaurant. At night we had supper with the Italian family upstairs. At 9 o'clock went to bed and at 10 p.m. got march order. We are leaving for Algicrs tomorrow at 9 a.m.

December 5 - Philippeville

We left for Algiers at 9 a.m. We decided to ride all day and night until we reached the outskirts of Algiers. The weather was good. [**Note**: *approximately 300 miles to Algiers.]*

US Army truck convoy in North Africa stopped for a meal. The officers are seated at small table while the enlisted men stand around.
Picture credit: https://www.ww2online.org/

December 6 - Algiers

We pulled into our bivouac area at 1 a.m. We slept in till 10 a.m. We pulled out of here at 2 p.m. and went to the 105 C.A.A.A 3rd B- Hq to stay for a couple of days.

***Note**: The reference is to the 105th Coastal Artillery Anti-Aircraft 3rd Battalion Headquarters.*

December 7 - Algiers

Rested all day. At night went to Algiers. We stopped at Red Cross and saw a movie.

December 8 - Algiers

Today I was on K.P. duty. It was an easy K.P. and I ate good. Went to bed early because of the cold weather.

December 9 - Algiers

Spent the day around the area. It was raining cats and dogs. At night went to a movie in town.

Soldiers in camp during rainy weather in North Africa, 1943

Picture credit: https://www.ww2online.org/image/soldiers-raincoats-camp-north-africa-1943

December 10 - Algiers

Still raining today. Another quiet day around camp. Went to town at night to the Red Cross and a movie.

December 11 - Algiers

Today we went to the GOR *[Gun Operations Room]* and took over operations at 1 o'clock. I worked to 12 midnight. Still raining.

December 12 - Algiers

Today worked in GOR from 8 to 4. At night went to the Red Cross and then a movie.

December 13 -Algiers

Worked in GOR from 8 to 4 P.M. It was raining on and off all day. At night went to a movie.

December 14 - Algiers

Today we started our regular shifts. I am on the 4 to midnight shift all this week. Today was a beautiful, sun shining day.

December 15 - Algiers

Not much doing today. We had a good practice mission with the 8/L. Weather was also good. Had some Scotch.

December 16 - Algiers

Not much doing today. Still working from 4 to 12. The weather was warm today. Went to the Red Cross for shower.

December 17 - Algiers

Slept all morning and rested until I went to work. We had two missions today.

December 18 - Algiers

Today was another warm day, but the nights are very cold. Had one plotting mission in GOR.

Example of plotting table used in WWII, in this case in Great Britain. Picture credit: https://museumofworldwarii.org/

December 19 - Algiers

Today we built new bunks. Rested most of the day. Still working 4 to 12. Was working the switchboard for about an hour.

December 20 - Algiers

This was my last day of the 4 to 12 shift. Not much doing today. Rested most of day.

December 21 - Algiers

Had two shots in the arm. Started working the 8 to 4 shift. Went to a movie at the Red Cross Empire theatre.

December 22 - Algiers

Today was a dull day. Had a plotting mission in afternoon and trained on and off.

December 23 - Algiers

Went on pass at 4 o'clock and went to a movie at the Empire. Saw "Cheers for Miss Bishop."

Movie poster from 1941 movie Cheers for Miss Bishop

Figure 1 *Picture credit:* *https://alchetron.com/Cheers-for-Miss-Bishop*

December 24 - Algiers

We started drinking at four. At eight, 16 bottles of wine were gone. Visited several bars in the neighborhood and then everything went black.

December 25 - Algiers

Christmas.

Had a nice hangover. Worked from 8 to 4. Went on pass at 4. Went to Red Cross and then to Empire Theatre. Saw a Radio Broadcast to the states and saw "This is the Army".

December 26 - Algiers

Another dull day. It rained most of the day. Played cards at night.

December 27 - Algiers

Went into town on pass. Saw 2 movies: "Sky is the Limit", and another. Last day on 8 to 4. Started working 12 to 8 at midnight.

December 28 - Algiers

Worked from midnight to eight but slept most of the night and slept all morning. In the afternoon, took it easy.

December 29 - Algiers

Went into town and tried to have my picture taken. Made an appointment for tomorrow. Saw the movie, "Bataan".

December 30 - Algiers

Slept all night and morning. In the afternoon had my picture taken. The photographer scared me to death. Took it easy all day.

December 31 - Algiers

New Year's Eve.

Went on pass and went to a movie in afternoon. Spent a couple of hours in the afternoon at the Red Cross. Came back to the battery and a party was going full blast. Had some beer and saw the New Year in. It was a real noisy New Year's here in Algiers. Stayed up to 1 o'clock listening to the radio playing popular songs of the past year.

Algiers 1944 Happy New Year postcard from PFC Haight's collection.

1944

By January 1944, PFC Haight had been in North Africa for over a year. He had spent yet another Thanksgiving and Christmas far from home and family. It is doubtful that he and his fellow soldiers imagined another eighteen months of war.

The Allied success in North Africa provided a springboard for the invasion of Sicily in July 1943 by the now-seasoned Allied troops. By October 1943, the Allies had also prevailed in Sardinia and Corsica. Allied airbases were established on these two islands to support bombing raids in northern Italy and southern France. The Allied victory in Sicily resulted in the Italian government's surrender to the Allies on 3 September 1943. However, Hitler then launched Operation Axis, the occupation of Italy—and the fighting continued.

With the capture of Naples in October 1943, the Allies controlled three of Italy's main ports, Naples, Bari, and Taranto. In July 1944, Caserta, an area near Naples, became the headquarters for the Allied Forces. However, the war in Italy was far from over, and the fight for the northern part of the country would prove protracted and costly.

These battles were yet to come for PFC Haight. As 1944 began, he remained in Algiers. In his role as an aircraft warning plotter, it is likely that the months he spent in Algiers in 1944 were in support of the Allied airbases in Sardinia and Corsica. As part of the 44th AAA Brigade under General Ralph Tobin, he at last left Algiers in July 1944, about the same time that the Allied Headquarters were moved from there to Caserta near Naples. The postcards that he sent home in July were from Sardinia.

From there, he moved with the 44th to Corsica. It was in Corsica that, since the need for anti-aircraft artillery (AAA) was diminishing as the enemy's air power was destroyed, 15-20,000 AAA troops were converted to Infantry and Field Artillery.

In September 1944, PFC Haight was sent to Rome. His assignment there is unknown. What is known (from an article written by General Tobin which appeared in the Coast Artillery Journal) is that, in November 1944, the 44th Brigade to which he belonged was assigned to the Sixth Army Group as part of the Infantry and sent to southern France—and the front lines.

Since PFC Haight's 1944 journal was lost at some time over the past decades, a rough sketch of his life and whereabouts—drawn from postcards, pictures, and military records—is provided on the following pages.

January 1944 – Algiers

January 5

Two pictures sent to PFC Haight's family dated January 5, 1944. The one below has the lighthearted message, "This is me and the pigeons. Love from all of us."

January 24

This program was found with PFC Haight's other war memorabilia. It is for a USO Armed Forces show starring actor George Raft held at the Algiers Opera House.

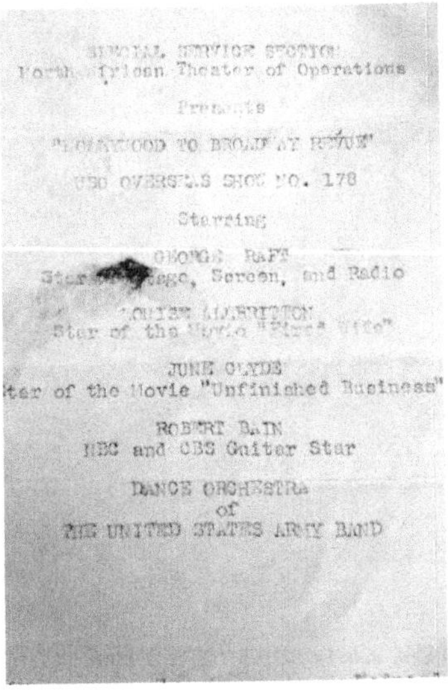

As numerous entries made throughout the journal show, the Red Cross and USO did much to support the troops who were living in primitive conditions amid uncertain and dangerous circumstances far from home.

March – Algiers

PFC Haight and two Army buddies pose for a picture in Algiers.

Since PFC Haight now had a regular work schedule, he had more time for sight-seeing. After the stress of plotting missions and tracking aircraft, there were long hours to fill and the need to focus on something besides missing family and home.

April – Algiers

Picture notation from PFC Haight: "Old Turkish building in the old Red Light District."
Note the military officers on the left and the Arab woman on the right.

Picture notation: "This is the courtyard of the building in picture [of the old Turkish building]. Oh, yes, that's me."

May – Algiers

In a webcast filmed in 2004 as part of the National World War II Reunion held on Memorial Day weekend in Washington, DC, Red Cross historian Brian Williams observed, "At the peak of activity in World War II, 7.5 million volunteers along with 40,000 paid staff provided services at home and abroad to over 16 million military personnel."

This interesting and informative webcast (https://www.loc.gov/item/webcast-8200) includes a presentation by Riki Belew, a volunteer whose first assignments were in Red Cross clubs for troops in North Africa. One of those clubs, Palm Beach, was about fifteen miles outside of Algiers. In May 1944, PFC Haight and a couple of his buddies spent some leave time at this club outside Algiers. Some of the pictures that he sent home are reproduced below.

"Here's a good picture of the three of us, Webb on the left, Schlosser, and me. It looks like I've got an awful high forehead in this one. The old hair is getting mighty thin."

"Here I am again in front of the bar room and again they cut the Palm Beach sign in half."

"This picture was taken from the top of the recreation villa. You can see part of the tennis court and next to that is the snack bar and that's Palm Beach."

June

Much has been written and many movies have been made about the June 6, 1944, invasion of Normandy, France on what has come to be called D-Day. The massive Allied invasion along the coast of Normandy included the largest amphibious landing force ever assembled. The fiercest fighting took place on Omaha Beach, where thousands of soldiers faced machine gun fire as they scaled cliffs on which the Germans had mounted their defenses. The successful invasion amid so much sacrifice (both military and civilian) resulted in the first significant presence the Allies had in Northern Europe since the retreat at Dunkirk in 1940.

Until the Allies won the North African campaign in May 1943 and established a foothold in southern Italy in September 1943, the Axis powers controlled all of North Africa (except Egypt) and much of continental Europe. A map of North Africa and Europe at the time would have shown Great Britain and Egypt as the only Allied countries. Given the battering that Great Britain was receiving from German bombers, it is clear that, had the US not joined the war in Europe, the world today would be a very different place from the one we know.

It is important to note that, although the Soviets were part of the Allied forces, the Western Allies were concerned (rightfully so, as it turned out) that the Soviets would not relinquish any territory that they captured. Therefore, the Western Allies focused on establishing a foothold in France before the Soviets could do so.

PFC Haight was in Algiers on D-Day. He left North Africa in July to support the battle for Northern Italy and the Alsace Lorraine region of France. He was part of the Allied force operations that came out of North Africa and headed through

Italy while other forces attacked from the French coast of Normandy, as shown on the map.

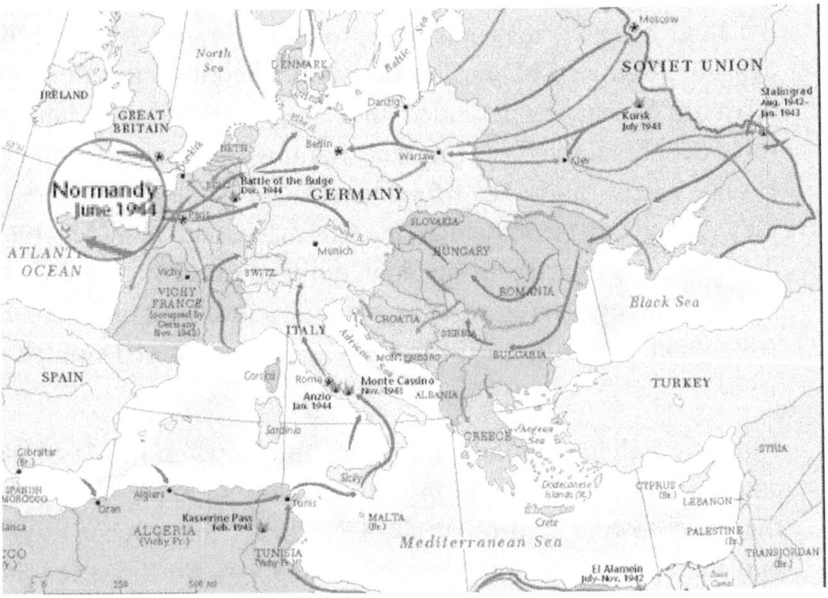

Picture credit: http://sites.austincc.edu/caddis/world-war-ii-1944-45

July – Sardinia

PFC Haight arrived on the island of Sardinia off the west coast of Italy in July.

While Axis forces were entrenched on the island, Sardinia was relentlessly bombed by Allied planes from 1940 through August 1943. The port and city of Cagliari suffered significant destruction, with more than 75% of its buildings destroyed. When Allied troops landed at Cagliari in September 1943, the Sardinians began returning to the bombed-out city.

Bombed-out city of Cagliari, Sardinia. Public domain - Wikipedia

To compensate for the loss of PFC Haight's record of his time in Sardinia, a portion of a memoir by a US Navy sailor, Milton W. Sherman (1919-2010), who arrived in late 1944 onboard the USS Denebola, is provided here. Sherman describes Sardinia as Haight and his fellow soldiers would have seen and experienced it.

> *Cagliari was perhaps the most pathetic of all the places at which we called. Pathetic because, even to us the place was not militarily significant. The trouble was that the Germans were, or had been using it as a transfer area for supplies. For that reason nearly one hundred American bombers came over some months before we were there and in their effort to bomb the waterfront and harbor, for the most part missed both and rained bombs on the city... Numerous were the church domes that had been shattered, and resembled huge broken eggshells.*

> *Cagliari...was a city of people who were obviously tired and weary of it all, and yet seemed to bear no ill-will to we Americans. It was here that we had our first exposure to the street urchins of Europe; Italy in particular. When they were not crying, "Hey, Joe, gimme money," or "Hey Joe, sella cigarretta?" they were pointing to bomb damage and repeating "Americano Bomba."*
>
> *These were the same kids who, while wallowing in the filth of the harbor...would fight each other tooth and nail for the Hershey bars that we attempted to scale from the ship to the jetty but usually missed and fell into the water. Often they would tear the candy to pieces until there was nothing left of it. They seemed to prize most highly the Hershey bars and any form of soap. To look at them was to understand why."* (Stephen Sherman, April, 2010. Updated February 16, 2012. http://acepilots.com/travel/cagliari.html)

Some vintage postcards of Cagliari accompanied the online publication of Navy Seaman Sherman's memoir.

PFC Haight also purchased some postcards. His messages on them, while light-hearted, hint at the devastation that he witnessed.

"Dearest Irene. Don't know what to write. Can't say much on a postcard. But all is well. Love, Alty"

"Dearest Irene. One of the many parks in this city.

Must have been nice in peace time. Love, Alty"

"Dearest Irene. If the place looked like this, it would be all right. Love, Alty"

Corsica

The Axis powers developed significant sea and land bases on Corsica, a French island off the northwestern coast of Italy. Their foothold was further entrenched after Allied bombing forced German troops to leave Sardinia for their positions in Corsica. The Corsican resistance, assisted by the Italian resistance, fought the German presence until, assisted by the Allies, Corsica was liberated in September 1943 in what was dubbed Operation Vesuvius.

This photo of Bastia, Corsica, shows the devastation of Saint Nicholas Square following fighting and numerous bombardments.
Picture credit:
https://dlockyer.wordpress.com/2015/05/08/liberation-of-corsica-1943

PFC Haight transferred from Sardinia to Corsica in the summer of 1944, as did Navy Seaman Sherman some months later. The latter wrote, *"Next was Ajaccio, Corsica, birthplace of Napoleon, and that was the only thing it had going for it. Unless one counts the bold and mangy rats that could be seen most any time scurrying along the gutter, darting in and out of alleys."*

Years later, in one of his rare references to his time as a soldier, Haight also mentioned the rats to his son, Robert.

However, as evidenced by his note on this postcard, some areas of Corsica remained untouched by the war.

"Dearest Irene,

This is one of the nicest little towns on the Island. I have visited it and enjoyed my stay there, even though a short one. Love Alty."

PFC Haight always maintained an upbeat tone in his messages home, never hinting at the realities of war.

September 1944 – Naples, Italy

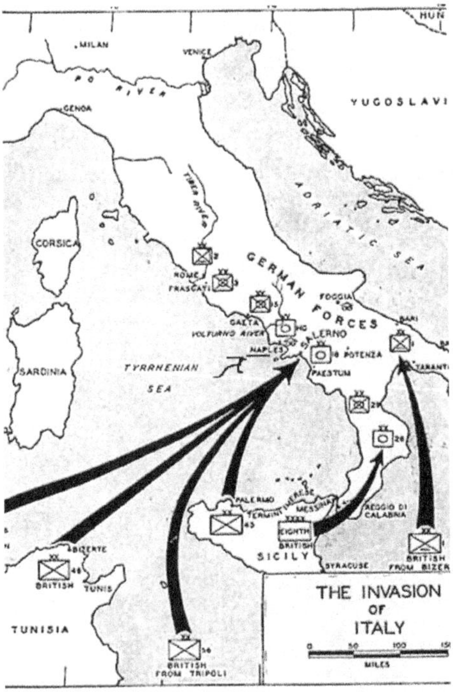

Allied bombing attacks on Naples began in 1940, with most occurring in 1943 after Sicily had been taken from the Germans. In September 1943, Allied forces landed on the coast of Italy and faced intense fighting but were able to capture the important port city of Naples on October 1, 1943. PFC Haight arrived there one year later.

The bombed-out port of Naples

Picture credit: National Archives

On his way to Rome in September 1944, PFC Haight flew from Corsica to Naples on a C-47 similar to the one shown in the picture below. This aircraft was used throughout the war to transport troops and supplies. By the time Haight arrived in Naples to spend the day, the city had been in Allied hands for 12 months.

Picture credit:
https://www.nationalww2museum.org/war/articles/douglas-c-47

On postcards sent home, PFC Haight wrote the following message to his wife using a number of separate postcards:

"Arrived here today, September 3. Spending the day here.

We flew over in a C-47. A very uneventful flight. Tomorrow we leave for Rome.

Not a bad place, but I walked my legs off today.

We have a room here in the city. You should see it. It looks like a stable, but it was all we could get. Plenty of gift shops here. Got mother a pin here, but will get more tomorrow.

I am travelling with two other fellows and we are taking plenty of pictures. Hope to get to Rome early tomorrow."

He also wrote in a postcard sent to his mother,

"We have a room here in the city and I am tired from walking my legs off in this city, but it was worth it."

Below are pictures of PFC Haight and his traveling companions on the day he spent in Naples.

Posing with an Italian guard

"Italian Guard Red & White uniform, Sgt Briteki and me."

"Sgt Briteki, Sgt Sromek and me."

Rome, Italy

The Allies fought a protracted battle for Italy in which Rome was naturally strategically important and so, despite its historical and religious significance, was bombed on a number of occasions in 1943 and 1944. In August 1943, after Italian King Victor Emmanuel and his government fled the city, the Germans took over. Before the Allies liberated the city in June 1944, more than 1000 members of Rome's Jewish community were sent to the concentration camp at Auschwitz. Even after the city fell, the war in Italy was far from over.

PFC Haight arrived in Rome in September 1944. It is unclear how long he spent there. However, the numerous pictures of his time in Rome, along with a variety of items like the Allied Soldiers' Souvenir Guide shown on the next page, suggest that he was there for more than a few days.

Benito Mussolini's balcony. "This is the building he made all his famous speeches from."

"Me at Mussolini's Forum. Tennis court in background."

"Taken in a B-25." ***Note:*** *No other comment appears on the photo, but the implication is that PFC Haight had the opportunity to fly in a B-25 bomber while he was in Rome.*

"Me, Sgt. Sromek on top of Castel St. Angelo"

"One of the many bridges across the Tiber River"

In November, PFC Haight, now part of the infantry, moved with the 44th Brigade to southern France. His specific movements from November through December 1944 are unknown.

1945

By January 1945, PFC Haight was supporting the frontline troops as part of the infantry in the Alsace Lorraine region of northeastern France on the German border. Much of this region was liberated in the fall of 1944. However, in January 1945, battles continued to rage in the north and south of the region, as the map below shows.

The thick dark line zigzagging lengthwise through the center of the map represents the locations of the British troops. The arrows at the top and the bottom indicate the location of the front line on January 3, 1945.

On January 3, PFC Haight was in Sarralbe (city was added to the original map to show his proximity to the front).

Picture credit: www2days.com.

Map: Alsace Lorraine Region of France – Operation Nordwind

The journal entries continue:

In 1945, PFC Haight did not make daily journal entries as he did in 1943, presumably because of the difficulties posed by the primitive winter living conditions and daily uncertainties of life at the front. Rather, he penned sporadic entries in the back of a tiny, battered address book

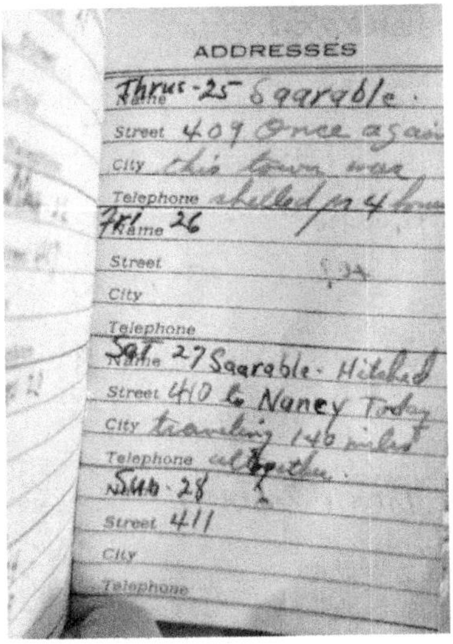

January 3 - Sarralbe, France

Tonight the Germans shelled this town hitting a building 500 yards away.

January 10 - Sarralbe

Today I was made a PFC *[Private First Class]*.

January 25 - Sarralbe

With 409 once again *[the 409th Infantry Regiment, which was part of 103rd Infantry Division of the 7th Army]*. This town *[Sarralbe]* was shelled for 4 hours.

Allied tank destroyers in Bettenhoffen moving toward Strasbourg to meet German forces near Sarralbe.

By January 25, the Allies controlled all of Alsace-Lorraine except for two small areas.

Picture credit: www2days.com

In bitter winter conditions, US infantrymen walk alongside a camouflaged tank during the Allied advance near Colmar south of Sarralbe in January 1945 as part of Operation Nordwind, which has been referred to as the "other Battle of the Bulge."

Picture credit: https://warfarehistorynetwork.com/

January 27 - Sarralbe

Hitched with 410 *[410th Infantry Regiment]* to Nancy today. Traveling 140 miles altogether.

Note: *Nancy, France is the capital city of the French region of Lorraine and the site of a 10 day battle in September 1944 where the US Army defeated German forces. The city then served as the garrison of Third Army HDQTRS providing the Allies with an important communications center.*

Soldiers sitting near a two-and-a-half-ton military cargo truck, France, 1945. PFC Haight would have traveled in a similar convoy of trucks and military vehicles.

Picture credit: https://www.ww2online.org/

February 22 - Dehlingen, France

This morning we moved 12 miles east *[of Sarralbe]* into the field. Living in tents *[in freezing, snowy, wet winter conditions]*.

A brother in arms:

> On February 21, 1945, PFC Haight's older brother, Army Staff Sergeant Robert Haight, landed in LeHavre, France on a troop ship from the States. SSG Haight was assigned to a company responsible for constructing bridges to allow the Seventh Army to cross large bodies of water—such as the Rhine River—at points where Allied bombing had destroyed bridges. In a document that he wrote for his family in 2003, he included his memories of the war. SSG Haight mentions that the route he traveled took him through Nancy, Reims, and Strasburg and then into Germany. Both he and his brother were supporting the Seventh Army. They passed through some of the same places, weeks apart, though they would not have known of each other's locations at the time. When the war ended, they were approximately 250 miles apart.
>
> From SSG Robert Haight's memories of the war: "Another very distinct memory I have of the war is going literally weeks without changing clothes or taking a shower…The last several weeks of the war in Europe, at least where I was, were almost complete chaos. The roads, narrow at best, were jammed with men, tanks and trucks of all kinds trying to move forward, while at the same time the Germans were

surrendering in large number and they had to be moved to the rear either on foot or by trucks on the same roads we were trying to use. The situation was made worse by the fact that German resistance was now not very strong, so the pace of the Army moving forward was stepped up considerably and it was difficult to keep vehicles fueled. It was also difficult to keep units together."

Seemingly endless lines of German prisoners and American supply trucks crossing the Rhine River in opposite directions on March 26, 1945, confirming SSG Haight's observations.

Picture credit: National Archives, US Army Signal Corps

Back to PFC Haight's journal:

March 7 - Dehlingen

Today we drew to go home. I lost and ended in 4th place.

March 13 – Dehlingen

7th Army offensive started today.

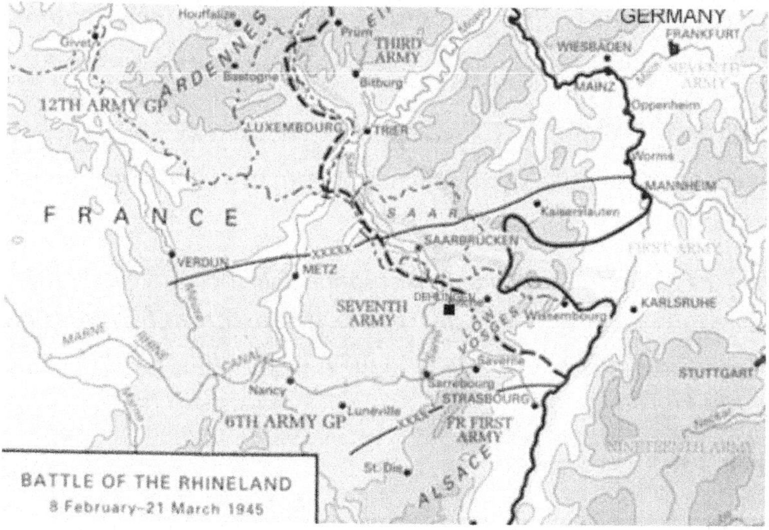

Picture credit: US Army Center of Military History
<u>https://history.army.mil/brochures/rhineland/rhineland.htm</u>

Dehlingen has been added to the map to show PFC Haight's location (in the middle just right of "SEVENTH ARMY." The dotted line indicates the front line on February 8 and the solid line indicates the front line on March 21. In its leading role in Operation Undertone, the 7th Army fought its way across the Rhine River into Germany. PFC Haight was very much in the middle of it.

March 17 - Rimling

We moved today at 1 this afternoon *[to Rimling, 12 miles from Dehlingen. The Army is slowly advancing.]* We are 2 miles from Germany.

March 18 - Rimling

We are out in the fields in tents. This town is a wreck of a ghost town. *[Rimling was site of a battle in January, and the fighting had continued].*

March 21- Schwarzen

Arrived today to this small town in Germany. It is located 10 miles north of Zweibrucken.

Note: *PFC Haight landed in Casablanca, Morocco in November 1942. After almost 2½ years, from Africa through Sardinia, Corsica, Italy, and France, he and his fellow soldiers made their way into Germany.*

March 23

Moved today to Wattenheim, 30 miles NE of Kaiserlautern

Note*: On March 20, the 319th Infantry seized Kaiserlautern without resistance.*

March 24 – 25

Moved today to Offstein – 8 miles west of the Rhine and the city of Worms.

The 7th Army 15th Corps started to cross the Rhine.

US Army crossing the Rhine at Worms on a heavy pontoon bridge in March 1945.

Remnants of the original bridge can be seen in the upper part of the picture. ***Note:*** *This is the type of bridge that PFC Haight's brother would have been involved in constructing.*
Public domain photo: https://commons.wikimedia.org/wiki

March 26 – near Worms

German planes flew over our position. 7 were shot down

Picture credit: https://i.redd.it/9zwqzz1i7qvy.jpg

March 27 - Worms on the Rhine

Moved here this afternoon. Living in a building.

Much of the city of Worms was destroyed. After sleeping in a pup tent or out in the elements, even a damaged building would have been an improvement.

Soldiers of the Third US Army, 4th Armored Division advance through rubble in Worms searching for Nazi snipers, March 20, 1945

Picture credit: https://wvhistoryonview.org/catalog/041175

March 31 -Worms

Today we discovered a wine cellar. Thousands of bottles of Champagne.

April 14 - Worms

Major Brown left this morning

April 18 - Worms

4 aircraft were over tonight. We claimed 2. No damage.

Photo of PFC Haight that may have been taken during this time.

Soldiers with the US 3rd Infantry Division in Nuremberg on April 20, 1945
Public domain photo:
https://en.wikipedia.org/wiki/Western_Allied_invasion_of_Germany

April 22 - Worms

Left Worms this morning. Stayed in a town 15 miles east of Wurzburg

April 23-24 near Wurzburg

Arrived today at our new position 18 miles south of Nurnberg *[Nuremberg]* and eight miles South of Schwabach. Our position is on a German airfield.

American infantrymen of the US 11th Armored Division supported by an M4 Sherman tank move through a smoke-filled street in Wernberg, Germany, April 1945.

Public domain photo: https://en.wikipedia.org/wiki/Western_Allied_invasion_of_Germany

April 25

Moved today. 25 miles south to a small town of Trecuhtiergen *[sic]*.

April 26

We are living in a farmhouse 30 miles north of the Danube River.

April 27

Moved today out on a hill a couple of 100 yards from the Danube River.

April 28

We are located near the small town of Altishein *[sic]* on the Danube River.

May 3 - 4

Moved this morning. Crossing the Danube and setting up in a small town 15 miles east of Munich. Living in a building.

May 5 – Salzburg, Austria

Moved today to Austria and set up in Salzburg *[about 90 miles from Munich]*.

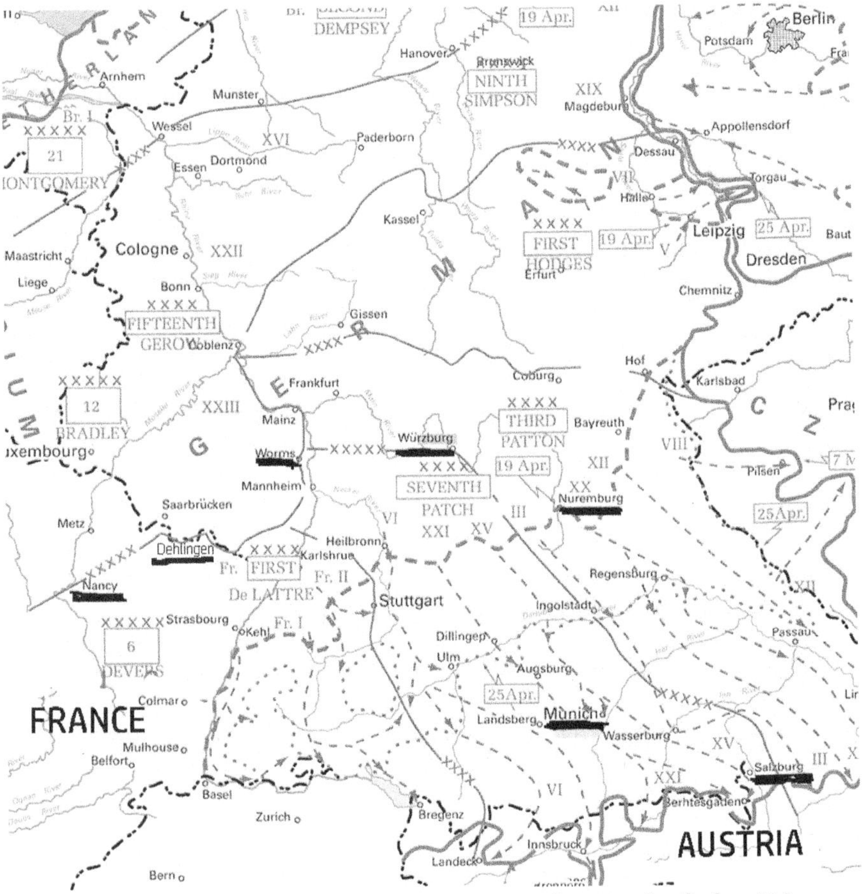

Portion of **Final Operations Map: The End of the War**

Map showing US Army movement from mid-April until the Germans surrendered on May 7. The dark underlining of cities shows PFC Haight's movements beginning in January.

January 27 – Nancy, February – Dehlingen, March – Worms, late April - Wurzberg and Nuremburg, May 3 - near Munich. May 5 - Salzburg, Austria
Berlin is in the upper right corner.

Picture credit: United States Military Academy Dept. of History

May 8 - Salzburg

V-E Day 12 noon *[Victory in Europe day]*

Left for Paris. Stayed night at Stuttgart. *[236 miles from Salzburg]*

Historical Background: *After Adolf Hitler committed suicide on April 30, his successor, Karl Donitz, negotiated an end to the war with the Allies, seeking to save Germany from the Soviets. On May 4, a German delegation arrived at British Field Marshal Montgomery's headquarters east of Hamburg to surrender forces in the Netherlands, northwestern Germany, and Denmark. Montgomery accepted the unconditional surrender of these troops.*

On May 7, at his headquarters in Reims, France, Supreme Allied Commander General Eisenhower accepted the unconditional surrender of all German forces.

The Soviets desired an official ceremony as well, so, on May 8, Chief of the Armed Forces High Command, Field Marshal Wilhelm Keitel signed Nazi Germany's unconditional surrender near Berlin.

Picture credit: https://www.bbc.com/news/world-europe-52572544

May 9

Left Stuttgart and went to Strasbourg *[100 miles away]* and took train to Paris *[about 250 miles away]*.

[PFC Haight and friends spent about 3 days celebrating in Paris.]

Paris pictures -

Haight and friends enjoy a drink.

Posing at a fountain.

May 13 - Paris

Left Paris tonight at 8:30 and riding 3rd class on the railroad.

May 14 - Strasbourg

Arrived in Strasbourg this morning at 10 and stayed overnight at Dachau.

***Note**: The concentration camp at Dachau was liberated on April 29. Since there is no reference to the camp, we can assume PFC Haight and his fellow soldiers passed through Dachau at a brisk pace without seeing or hearing about the camp.*

May 16 – June 12 Salzburg

[No entries other than header note: Salzburg]

June 13 - Salzburg

Today I was told I start for home on the 18th.

June 15 - Salzburg

Moved today to Straubing *[approximately 90 miles from Salzburg]*.

Now in the 3rd Army

June 18 - Straubing

Left the 44th this morning and started for Home.

June 19 - Mannheim, Germany *[300 miles from Straubing]*

Left here today for Thionville, France

June 20-21 - Thionville, France *[137 miles from Mannheim]*

We are here for 10 days and with the 466REINFCo 82nd br APO 583.

Here just for processing.

June 29

Left tonight at 9 for Marseilles.

June 30

On the road riding in 4048.

July 1 - Sunday

Arrived at the staging area 15 miles outside of Marseilles *[approximately 500 miles from Thionville]*

This is the final entry.

***

Demobilization and the return home

Many decades after the war, Alty Haight's memory was jogged when he viewed the WWII exhibits in the Smithsonian's Air and Space Museum in Washington DC. He mentioned to family members that he had been given the opportunity to return home by plane after the war. His friends and fellow soldiers traveled home by troopship—a much slower method of travel. His flight home was a reward, an honor for some unexplained action. That plane ride expedited his return to his family—a reunion with his wife and an opportunity to meet Kathleen, his three-year-old daughter.

The demobilization effort faced by the military at the end of the war is mind-boggling to consider. In May 1945, the US had more than 12 million men and women in the armed forces, 7.6 million of them stationed abroad, with 5.8 million in the Army and Army Air Force. Three million were in Europe.

However, not all of these Army and Army Air Force personnel were scheduled to return to the United States at the end of the war in Europe. Some stayed on as an occupying force, and about one million were to be sent to the Pacific to continue fighting. After Japan surrendered in August, those still awaiting transport to the Pacific became part of the demobilization back to the United States.

Some 2.25 million soldiers in Europe were scheduled for discharge from May 1945 through December 1946, creating a massive problem for the military as it sought to send them home as quickly as possible. Many, like my father-in-law, had been away from their families for three or more years.

Assembly areas large enough to accommodate 310,000 soldiers were established in France. These soldiers lived in tent cites while awaiting transport home. For many months, ship transports to the US averaged more than 435,000 soldiers per month.

Reference: https://www.wikiwand.com/en/ and https://en.wikipedia.org/wiki/Demobilization_of_United_States_armed_forces_after_World_War_II

This photo of PFC Haight (third from left) and friends might have been

taken in the tent city near Marseilles while they awaited transport home.

In his memoir, General Eisenhower noted that troops were complaining about how long it was taking them to return to the States. Once, when he asked a large gathering of soldiers whether they preferred to fill the ships at normal capacity or instead be "crammed the hell into them" to get home as soon as possible, they applauded the latter option!

The picture below shows that Eisenhower granted their request.

A packed ship bringing American troops home in 1945. They are crowding the rails as the ship pulls into harbor. The voyage from Europe took 5 to 7 days.

Ships like the Queen Elizabeth could carry 15,000 troops and 900 crew members.

Picture and text credit: https://rarehistoricalphotos.com/

***

Private First Class Alton Haight was discharged from the US Army on July 16, 1945 at Fort Dix, New Jersey, two weeks after his arrival at the staging center in France on July 1.

From the military separation papers of Alton Shaw Haight:

Battles and campaigns: Central Europe, Northern France, Rhineland, Southern France

Decorations and Citations: European-African-Middle Eastern Service Medal, Good Conduct Medal

AFTERWORD

If I had attempted to create this book just a few years ago, I would have had to meet with research librarians, travel to military libraries, and visit the National Archives in Washington, DC. Thanks to the Internet, however, I was able to retrieve significant details with a few keystrokes. Through long hours at my computer, I located information, pictures, and maps detailing the many Army operations (with such names as Torch, Strike, Husky, and Undertone) that impacted PFC Haight's life as a soldier in North Africa, Italy, France, and Germany from November 1942 to June 1945.

It was important to me that I find just the right photos to help tell the story—to provide a visual context for the spare words written by a young soldier in a tiny journal. Frustration piled upon frustration as I pulled the threads to unravel the complex and seemingly endless number of WWII internet entries. Sometimes, I had to settle for something less than what I sought, but I was always overwhelmed by what I learned. After my research, I came away with a sense of awe at the magnitude of the undertaking managed by General Eisenhower as Supreme Commander of the Allied Expeditionary Force in Europe.

My goal was to add detail to my father-in-law's journals and immerse the reader in the daily world of one man—one soldier among millions of soldiers. PFC Haight was one ordinary man like the millions of other ordinary men called upon to take up arms to save the world from the horrors wrought by Adolf Hitler in Europe. Whether or not I have been successful in that endeavor is for the reader to judge.

However, what cannot be denied is the sacrifice that they all made—especially those soldiers who paid the ultimate price and lost their lives fighting in a foreign land. I had always appreciated their sacrifice, but it was from a more distant place. Now, as a result of the education that I obtained in putting this book together, I feel a more personal sense of gratitude. For that, I am indebted to my father-in-law, Alton Shaw Haight, for leaving us his memories and his memorabilia, which served as the foundation for my curiosity and the springboard for my educational journey.

I appreciate receiving feedback from readers about my books. Please contact me through my website: www.ritamboehm.com, my Facebook page, @ Author Rita Boehm, or by leaving a review on www.amazon.com.

Thank you for taking this journey with me.

Rita M. Boehm

ACKNOWLEDGEMENTS

I am grateful to the following individuals for the information, support, assistance, and insight they provided—all of which greatly assisted me in the development of this book.

Irving Locker, WWII veteran – My afternoon meeting with this vibrant and personable 96-year-old was both informative and inspirational. Reviewing the Powerpoint presentation about his war service, viewing his collection of memorabilia, and listening to his experiences as part of an anti-aircraft artillery battery that landed on Utah Beach on D-Day gave me a better understanding of both the armament and the structure of an Army battery and further clarified the role that my father-in-law played in the war.

Donn Dears – author of *The Looming Energy Crisis* and a fellow member of the Writers League of The Villages, read through the first draft of the book. His detailed comments allowed me to address a number of areas that required clarification or correction.

Steven Haight – son of SSG Robert Haight, shared his father's memories of the war and helped me round out my father-in-law's story by including his brother's war service.

James Renner – a member of the WWII Book Club of The Villages, generously gave his time to read and offer comments on the first draft of the book. He also provided a much-appreciated introduction to Irving Locker.

Any inaccuracies, oversights, and mistakes made in the telling of my father-in-law's story are entirely my own.

Throughout this book, picture and text credit is noted where due. Following below, in alphabetical order, are the primary research sites used in the book's development:

- Australian War Memorial: https://www.awm.gov.au/collection/C331072
- Coast Artillery Journal, May-June 1948, Activities of the 44th AAA Brigade, Brigadier General Ralph C. Tobin
- Encyclopedia Britannica: www.Britannica.com
- History of Personnel Demobilization in the United States Army, John C. Sparrow, https://history.army.mil/html/books/104/104-8/CMH_Pub_104-8.pdf
- History Hub: http://sites.austincc.edu/caddis/world-war-ii-1944-45
- History Net: https://www.historynet.com
- Military.com: https://www.military.com/daily-news
- Museum of World War II: https://museumofworldwarII.org
- National Archives
- National World War 2 Museum: https://www.nationalww2museum.org
- US Army Center of Military History
- Rare Historical Photos: https://rarehistoricalphotos.com
- War History Online: https://www.warhistoryonline.com
- Warfare History Network: https://warfarehistorynetwork.com
- Wikipedia (in its many incarnations)
- World War 2 Days: www2days.com
- World War 2 Online: https://www.ww2online.org

Made in the USA
Coppell, TX
23 May 2021

56191400R00098